THE DIALECTIC
OF IMMATERIALISM

An account of the making of Berkeley's *Principles*

The *Philosophical Commentaries*, folio 105 recto, entries nos. 15–27.
(The pencil scorings are not by Berkeley.)

THE DIALECTIC
OF IMMATERIALISM

An account of the making
of Berkeley's *Principles*

By

A. A. LUCE, M.C., D.D., Litt.D.

Berkeley Professor of Metaphysics
in the University of Dublin

HODDER AND STOUGHTON

London

CONTENTS

5

PREFACE

BERKELEY's *Principles of Human Knowledge* was five or six years in the making. The documented story of the build-up of its main argument is told in the following pages. Minor supporting arguments and literary details are not stressed. I have concentrated on the dialectical development of Berkeley's immaterialism, as he turned its key doctrines over and over in his mind prior to publication. Our chief source-material is the pair of notebooks, now known as Berkeley's *Philosophical Commentaries*.

Berkeley's notebooks have a good deal in common with those of Wittgenstein. Both sets have authorship in view, and contain notes for projected books. Either set sheds light on the growth and march of its author's thought. Both men were lonely thinkers, as they filled their notebooks, wrestling with stubborn problems. Both rise easily from homely conceits to speculative heights. Both were deeply interested in language and thought, in words and signs, and both experimented in wordless thinking. Both wrote on sense-impressions and physical objects, on the understanding and the will, on doubt and certainty, on voluntary movement of legs and arms, and even on vanishing chairs. Wittgenstein had it in mind, he says, to "publish those old thoughts and the new ones together", because the new ones could be seen in the right light only "against the background of my old way of thinking". Here the parallel is very close; for Berkeley's "second thoughts", as he called them, can be seen in the right light only against the background of his old way of thinking, that he called "my first arguings".

As a series Berkeley's notes are relatively compact. Coming to the *Philosophical Commentaries* fresh from reading the *Philosophical Investigations* or the *Blue Book* or the *Brown*, one feels the self-discipline of Berkeley's preparations for authorship, and the point, purpose and method of his preliminary studies. Both men "jump from one topic to another"; yet Berkeley's eight hundred and eighty-eight notes, practically all of them, are connected by invisible threads to "ye immaterial hypothesis", named on line 7 of our frontispiece which reproduces folio 105*r*.

This reproduction repays close study. It shows a specimen page of the notebooks typical of all the pages, and it contains, if not my case in a nutshell, at least ocular evidence for the essentials. Here can be seen the lay-out and pattern of the one hundred and fifty-two folios, filled with the notes or "entries", all separate. Berkeley treated the entries with the respect an author shows to galley-proofs, correcting, amplifying, annotating. The marginal apparatus of letters and signs deserves special attention. It runs from the first page to the last, unifying the work, and rendering the notebooks serviceable to the author and to us. One glance at it showed me years ago that these were not collections of odd jottings, as at first they were supposed to be. The notebooks are obviously a methodical composition; they look two ways, like the heraldic eagle. The notes are a stage in the making of the *Principles*, midway between Berkeley's first writings on immaterialism and his published work. By means of this apparatus Berkeley indexed his notes and sorted them out, linking some to the *Principles*, some to the *Essay on Vision* and consigning some to the scrap-heap.

Those on the scrap-heap are of peculiar significance, like the stones from the river Jordan. Pieced together and assembled round the fourth note from the foot of our frontispiece, these discarded notes tell a tale, hitherto neglected or unknown. They tell of the young thinker's drastic revision of his original thesis, and of a dramatic change in his mood and mode of approach. They lay bare the secret dialectic of Berkeley's immaterialism. They tell how the fantastic theosophy, sketched on this opening page, was cut and slashed and pruned by its author till it grew or was shaped into the sober philosophy he published.

Pioneer work on these notebooks was done by A. C. Fraser, G. A. Johnston, myself and others. The present study takes up just where my *editio diplomatica* of 1944 left off. It reads between the lines, as well as on them. It attempts to trace systematically the key doctrines of the *Principles*, viz. Berkeley's teaching on matter, existence, abstraction, body and mind, from their main source in Continental scepticism through the *Philosophical Commentaries* to the beginning of the drafting of the published work in the late autumn of 1708. If my account proves to be correct and convincing, it should help to bury those caricatures and tragic perversions of Berkeley's philosophy that trace largely to Reid and Beattie, and to Kant; it confirms broadly, I think, the interpretation, reached independently by Professor T. E. Jessop and myself, and reflected in our edition of the *Works*.

The numbering of the entries is that given in Volume I of the *Works*, which was taken over from the edition of 1944. The entries quoted are printed distinctively in italics with their marginal signs or letters, and with Berkeley's spelling, punctuation and capitals.

I am grateful to my colleagues, Mr. F. La T. Godfrey and Professor E. J. Furlong, for much kind help, and not least for their criticisms and advice, which I have always valued, but not, I fear, always heeded.

A. A. LUCE
Trinity College, Dublin
November 1962

CHAPTER I

THE REVISION

BERKELEY's *Principles* was published in May 1710, after (the Preface says) "a long and scrupulous inquiry". The inquiry covered probably five or six years, and the climax of it was the drastic revision Berkeley carried out in 1707–8. It was a revision of the basic doctrines of the "immaterial hypothesis". The work of the revision was done in the two notebooks, now known as the *Philosophical Commentaries*. Our principal task is to examine those notebooks in detail, and to show from the entries the steps and stages of the revision, tracing the sinuous development of Berkeley's thought in this his "wonder-year". We shall be occupied with his change of views, kaleidoscopic at times, on the basis of immaterialism, on the nature and meaning of existence, on abstract general ideas, on the reality of body, on person, consciousness and mind, and on the concept of deity. In Chapters II, III and IV, by way of introduction and explanation, I have given short accounts of Berkeley's method, of his early writings, and of his main authorities, Locke, Malebranche and Bayle. The present chapter is mainly concerned with the external evidence for the revision, namely Berkeley's own statements about it, and about his change of views.

The results of the revision by and large were final, and they are embodied in the published works. The revision has therefore a direct bearing on Berkeleian interpretation today, and our study of it is far from being a literary luxury. In studying the *making* of the *Principles* we are getting to know the teaching of the *Principles*. Readers who are puzzled by, for instance, his statements about the external world and are anxious to know what Berkeley really did mean, are bound to be helped by knowing what Berkeley had held about the external world, and had ceased to hold, thanks to the revision. On disputed points the revision is always a clue, and is often the key. To know what Berkeley's problems were when his philosophy was in the making, to be able to look over his shoulder as he seeks and finds his solutions, in a word to watch the reviser revising— these are great aids to students of his thought. Had the truth about the making of the *Principles* been known to scholars of an earlier day, Berkeleian exegesis must have taken a different course. Had Reid and Beattie, Kant and John Stuart Mill seen the documents that we can see, had they known about the revision what we may know, they could not have written about Berkeley as they did; and the stereotyped picture of the man and his teaching given in many histories of philosophy would have been other than it is.

Here is an epitome of the broad facts that concern us. During the years 1704–6 Berkeley constructed an immaterialist system which in retrospect he called "my first arguings"; in the summer and autumn of 1707 he placed that system in the melting-pot; he examined critically his first writings and first views; he rejected much, altered much, discovered much. By the autumn of 1708 his "second thoughts" (to use his own phrase) were more or less complete and systematized. He had found a new way of disproving the existence of matter. He had returned to a common-sense belief in the existence of body and the world of sense. He had profoundly modified his conception of mind, and had broadened and deepened his conception of deity.

It was a radical change of view and viewpoint, amounting to an intellectual conversion. It issued in a thorough re-shaping and re-writing of the original thesis. Berkeley called it a *revision*, but he also called it a *revolt*.* It went far deeper than a revision usually goes, as one sees by comparing it with Berkeley's revision for the second (1734) edition of the *Principles*.† Berkeley's revision of 1734 was stylistic and literary; it made no

---

* See below, p. 16, and the *Works of George Berkeley* (Luce and Jessop), Vol. II, p. 172.

† Summarized in Appendix III below.

alteration of doctrine. His revision of 1707–8 was intellectual surgery; it altered the character of the immaterial hypothesis.

Berkeley himself was well aware of the importance of his intellectual conversion and he wished his readers to know of it. He announced it, in effect, as is shown below, and described its general character at the very beginning of both his main works on immaterialism, explicitly in the *Three Dialogues*, obliquely in the *Principles*. He referred to it again and illustrated it with a vivid simile at the close of the *Three Dialogues*. He mentioned it as an important matter in the letter to Sir John Percival, quoted and discussed below (p. 20); and further sidelights on the revision are contained in his other letters of the period.

In 1710 Berkeley came before the public with a new book, and he came with the revision uppermost in his mind, if we may judge from its opening section. Three years later he brought out another book, and again the revision is given prominence at the outset. These are striking facts. Berkeley was an innovator, and he knew it. He had a challenging creed to propound; but before the novelty and the challenge he placed the thought of his careful revision. It is as if he wished to inspire his readers with the spirit of caution. Aware of the intrinsic difficulties of immaterialism, alive to the dangers on the right hand and the left, he prefixed a warning notice, as it were. He knew from his own experience that immaterialism is easily misunderstood, and that first thoughts about it must be checked with second thoughts.

We begin with the passage about the *revolt*, quoted below from the opening of the *Three Dialogues*. Written in the first person singular, it is obviously a dramatization of Berkeley's personal experience. The corresponding passage in the *Principles*, as befits a sober *treatise*, begins in the third person plural and its personal character is disguised; but it ends in the first person plural, and as soon as it is read in the light of the passage from the *Dialogues* with attention to the repetition of thought and phrase, it too is at once seen to be the author's personal experience generalized. In other words, in accordance with his usual practice, Berkeley has modelled the opening of the *Dialogues* on the opening of the *Principles*, and both passages refer to the revision and the intellectual mutation that went with it.

In the first dialogue the curtain goes up on a peaceful scene. Philonous, the friend of mind, and Hylas, the champion of matter, are chatting amicably in a sheltered garden at dawn of day; they are watching the purpling sky, listening to bird-song, scenting the fragrance of trees and flowers, and feeling "the gentle influence of the rising sun". Their senses are all engaged with sensible realities, and their spirits are keyed to a great adventure in the world of thought. The stage is set. They will soon be at it, hammer and tongs; but at the moment all is sweetness, harmony and peace.

Hylas sets the ball a-rolling. He speaks out against two things, paradoxes and scepticism, condemning those who pretend "either to believe nothing at all, or to believe the most extravagant things in the world". He has Philonous in mind, or what he has heard of Philonous, and he expects violent disagreement; to his great surprise he encounters agreement. Philonous who always voices Berkeley's views, Philonous who *is* Berkeley dramatized, expresses complete agreement with Hylas on both points, condemning "affected doubts" and "fantastical conceits". He drives it home and clinches his words with the following personal statement:

> PHILONOUS. I am even so far gone of late in this way of thinking, that I have quitted several of the sublime notions I had got in their schools for vulgar opinions. And I give it you on my word, since this revolt from metaphysical notions to the plain dictates of Nature and common sense, I find my understanding strangely enlightened, so that I can now easily comprehend a great many things which before were all mystery and riddle.

This is autobiography, pure and simple, true to fact, accurately phrased and dramatized. Berkeley has here given us a piece of his own intellectual history that was vital in the making of the

Principles. The "sublime notions" and "fantastical conceits" were those of Malebranche; the "affected doubts" were those of Bayle and the continental sceptics. Both sources left their mark on Berkeley's early work, and the two strains are not opposed. Indeed in some continental schools through the influence of Montaigne religion and scepticism, faith and philosophic doubt went hand in hand, and a measure of scepticism was used to defend the faith. Berkeley was deeply impressed by the sublime notions of Malebranche, and he made some of them his own. He accepted from Malebranche the immaterial hypothesis, sense symbolism, the passivity of unthinking things, the doctrine of the one true Cause, and, in part, the vision of all things in God. Then he met Pierre Bayle's dictionary. Bayle showed him that there are stronger arguments against matter than those Malebranche had used.* Berkeley swallowed the bait. He made use of these arguments, went some way with Bayle, and was confirmed in his immaterialism. Then the reaction set in. He saw the precipice ahead. He saw that his first method of disproving the existence of matter, which he learned from Malebranche, led to scepticism and played the game of Bayle. *Non tali auxilio*, he said to himself; thoroughly alarmed, he decided to examine and revise his first arguings, and to seek a surer foundation for immaterialism and a safer line of proof.

"I have quitted *several*† of the sublime notions I had got in their schools." He did not quit them all. Berkeley never denied his debt to Malebranche, and he recognized it in more ways than one. He visited Malebranche once, if not twice, on his first stay in Paris. He names Malebranche fourteen times in the *Commentaries*, in criticism every time; and those criticisms prove the extent and depth of the original debt. The *Three Dialogues* contains a long paragraph, inserted in the third edition (1734), designed to show that "upon the whole there are no principles more fundamentally opposite than his and

* See below, p. 67.
† Italics mine.

mine"—which is quite true *upon the whole*. But the passage *without the insertion*, i.e. as it appears in the first and second editions, is an expression of agreement with Malebranche on a central point.*

Berkeley's attitude to Malebranche was selective. He retained immaterialism, but gave it a different character and a different basis. He retained the vision of all things in God in its plain Pauline sense, but quitted or rejected the scholastic embroidery. He retained panentheism, but quitted panpsychism. He accepted much of Malebranche's doctrine of cause, but not all. He accepted the sole causality of spirit; but rejected the *occasion* and the automatism of human action. On the relativity and subjectivity of the sensible qualities, on judgments of sense, on sense-symbolism, and on the sensible as the language of the Author of Nature, Berkeley followed where Malebranche led.

There is then not the slightest doubt that Berkeley in his plastic period adopted notions from Malebranche, sublime and otherwise, and quitted several of them; nor can there be any reasonable doubt that the passage at the opening of the *Three Dialogues* refers to the early period in his development when he was strongly under the influence of Malebranche and Bayle, and was thoroughly sceptical about the existence of the world of sense.

What then was the "revolt" that led to the revision? Berkeley tells us quite plainly in this passage. It was a quitting of sublime notions for *vulgar opinions*. It was a "revolt from metaphysical notions to the plain dictates of Nature and common sense". Berkeley is asking us to believe that the turning-point in his preparatory work for the *Principles*† and the starting-point of the revision were, or at least involved, a return from a speculative flight to common sense. There is no difficulty in

---

* See *Works*, Vol. II, p. 214, and below, p. 187.

† The *Three Dialogues* is what it claims to be—an *exposition* of the doctrine of the *Principles*, and no more; and it is perfectly clear that the gist of this passage is identical with the gist of the first section of the Introduction to the *Principles*.

accepting this return of Berkeley's to vulgar opinions and common sense, when one knows the background of his books, as I hope to show. But it is not easy to convince folk that Berkeley teaches common sense; and there lie the difficulty and the importance of the study on which we are engaged.

When the evidence of the notebooks has been marshalled, readers will see clearly that Philonous's confession is not a literary façade; but is the honest utterance of Berkeley's hard-won personal experience. Every item in it can be checked and confirmed. Berkeley did embrace immaterialism under the influence of Malebranche and along Malebranchian lines. He did go some distance with Bayle along the sceptic's road; he did doubt the existence of body and the world of sense; he did doubt the existence of mind; and he did start back in intellectual fear when he saw what lay ahead. He did revolt from certain high-flying speculations; it was a metaphysician's revolt from metaphysics. He did return to certain vulgar opinions; it was a philosopher's return to common sense.*

The *Three Dialogues* closes as it began: "common sense" are the very last words; and the disputants endorse Philonous's opening statement, considered above; they do more; they corroborate it and fill in the detail by mentioning the Academics and Cartesians. Hylas, the materialist, if not converted, is not far from it; for a new light has broken in on his understanding; he is now convinced that he sees things as they are, and no longer worries about their unknown natures or absolute existence.

HYLAS. ... You set out upon the same principles that Academics, Cartesians, and the like sects, usually do; and for a long time it looked as if you were advancing their philosophical *scepticism*; but in the end your conclusions are directly opposite to theirs.

PHILONOUS. You see, Hylas, the water of yonder fountain, how it is forced upwards, in a round column, to a certain

---

* Berkeley was alive to the significance of these apparent paradoxes, and he explains clearly the truth shared between philosophers and the vulgar in *Principles*, sect. 56, and the *Three Dialogues*, *Works*, Vol. II, p. 262.

height; at which it breaks and falls back into the basin
from whence it rose: its ascent as well as descent, proceeding from the same uniform law or principle of *gravitation*.
Just so, the same principles which at first view lead to *scepticism*, pursued to a certain point, bring men back to common
sense.

Here Berkeley in the person of Philonous accepts the verdict
on the origin and early course of his philosophy, and points it
by a memorable image. The rising column of water makes one
think of his first attempt to establish immaterialism by aid of a
soaring metaphysic, and the falling column must refer to the
sudden change of direction and his return to common sense.

With these two passages in mind from the beginning and the
end of the *Three Dialogues* turn back now to the *Principles*. In the
first section of the Introduction we read:

". . . Yet so it is we see the illiterate bulk of mankind that
walk the high-road of plain, common sense, and are governed
by the dictates of Nature, for the most part easy and un-
disturbed. . . . They complain not of any want of evidence
in their senses, and are out of all danger of becoming *sceptics*.
But no sooner do we depart from sense and instinct to follow
the light of a superior principle, to reason, meditate, and
reflect on the nature of things, but a thousand scruples
spring up in our minds. . . . Prejudices and errors of sense do
from all parts discover themselves to our view; and endeav-
ouring to correct these by reason we are insensibly drawn
into uncouth paradoxes, difficulties, and inconsistences,
which multiply and grow upon us as we advance in speculation; till at length, having wander'd through many intricate
mazes, we find our selves just where we were, or, which is
worse, sit down in a forlorn scepticism."

When we compare the drift of the two passages and note the
common phraseology—the paradoxes, the dictates of nature
and plain common sense—there can be no doubt that Berkeley
has here followed his usual practice, and modelled the passage

in the *Dialogues* on that of the *Principles*, adding dramatic touches, and making explicit its basis in personal experience. All the features of Berkeley's intellectual odyssey are present in the opening section of the *Principles* as in the Dialogues. With the vulgar he walks the highroad of plain common sense; he obeys the dictates of nature, has confidence in his senses, and is in no danger of turning sceptic. Then comes the awakening. His peace of mind is rudely shaken by the superior principle of reason. Doubts and scruples about the evidence of sense spring up. He is drawn into uncouth paradoxes, and wanders through intricate mazes of speculation. Finally comes the *dénouement*. He must choose between sitting down "in a forlorn scepticism" and returning home just where he was before. He returns home.

The same intellectual odyssey and the same return home are vividly pictured in the following note, written by Berkeley on folio 4 of the notebook which is now classed as Add. MS. 39304 in the British Museum:

> "My speculations have the same effect as visiting foreign countries, in the end I return where I was before, set my heart at ease, and enjoy my self with new satisfaction."

Very close echoes of that note are contained in the seventh paragraph of the Preface of the *Three Dialogues*.

We pass on to a private letter of the period in which Berkeley made an important statement about the revision, and shows how he felt towards it. The letter is little known; it was discovered and published some fifty years ago by B. Rand,* but too late for Fraser's editions, too late to have its due influence upon the course of Berkeleian criticism. Owing to its early date, the circumstances of its writing, the feeling Berkeley has put into it, and the statements he makes in it about the revision and the doctrine of the *Principles*, the letter is source-material of the first rank.

Here are the circumstances. On 26 August 1710 Sir John Percival wrote from London to Berkeley in Dublin giving him

* B. Rand, *Berkeley and Percival* (Cambridge, 1914), pp. 80–5.

a report on the reception accorded in London to the *Principles*, published in Dublin in May of that year. The report was a bitter pill for the young author. The London wits would not take him seriously; they would not even read him; they ridiculed "the name" of his book; it denied the existence of matter; that was enough for them; they condemned it unread. They went on to discuss the author. He must be mad, said a physician, and ought to take remedies. He must be vain and insincere, said a bishop. Erasmus wrote in praise of folly, said a third; let this youngster exercise his wit; he is not so far gone as a gentleman in town, who asserts that we have no being at all.

Berkeley was stung to the quick. Without losing his temper or his dignity, and with proper thanks to Sir John for conveying the unwelcome news, on 6 September 1710 he launched out into a long and impassioned reply. It is a *cri de cœur*, quite unlike his ordinary calm and quiet style. Its emphatic character and solemn undertone are remarkable. There is nothing like it in his forty years' correspondence with his friend. After acknowledging Percival's efforts on his behalf, and desiring him, in speaking of the book, to dwell on its more positive teaching, and to leave its denial of matter to "steal unawares on the reader", Berkeley continues:

"Two imputations there are which (how unjust soever) I apprehended would be charged on me by censorious men, and I find it has happened accordingly. The first, that I was not myself convinced of the truth of what I writ, but from a vain affectation of novelty designed imposing on the world:— whereas there is nothing I esteem more mean and miserable, I may add more wicked, than an intention to cheat men into a belief of lies and sophisms merely for the sake of a little reputation with fools. God is my witness that I was, and do still remain, entirely persuaded of the non-existence of matter, and the other tenets published along with it. How desirous soever I may be to be thought well of, yet I hardly think that anyone in his wits can be touched with a vanity to distinguish himself among wise men for a mad man. This methinks should satisfy others of my sincerity at least, and that nothing less than a full conviction not only of the truth of my notions but also of their usefulness in the most important points, could have engaged me to make them public. I may add that the opinion of matter I have entertained some years; if therefore a motive of vanity could have induced me to obtrude falsehoods on the world, I had long since done it when the conceit was warm in my imagination, and not have staid to examine and revise it both with my own judgment and that of my ingenious friends.

"The second imputation I was afraid of is, that men rash in their censures, and that never considered my book would be apt to confound me with the sceptics, who doubt of the existence of sensible things and are not positive as to any one truth, no not so much as their own being (which I find by your letter is the case of some wild visionists now in London), but whoever reads my book with due attention will plainly see that there is a direct opposition betwixt the principles contained in it and those of the sceptics, and that I question not the existence of anything that we perceive by our senses."*

Berkeley has here answered two anticipated charges, the charge of insincerity and the charge of scepticism. In his reply to the former charge there are three points to notice: (1) his solemn, unequivocal declaration, made with God as witness, that he was, and remains, entirely persuaded of the non-existence of matter and of his other published tenets, (2) his statement that he had entertained the opinion of matter for some years, and (3) his argument that had he written out of vanity, he would have rushed into print when the conceit was warm in his imagination; whereas on the contrary he had stayed to examine and revise it, (a) with his own judgment, and (b) with that of his ingenious friends.

On these points I must observe that the solemn declaration

* *Works*, Vol. VIII, pp. 36–7.

covers not only the denial of the existence of matter but also the assertion of the existence of sensible things, which is specifically mentioned in the reply to the other charge. If then words mean anything, and if there are such things as veracity and religious conviction, it is utterly impossible to hold that Berkeley was sincere in denying the existence of matter, and insincere in asserting the existence of sensible things. He was sincere in both utterances.

On Berkeley's statement that for "some years" he had entertained the opinion of matter, let me comment that at least five or six years must have elapsed between his first conception of the "immaterial hypothesis" and the publication of the *Principles*. His examination of the thesis and the revision "with his own judgment" consisted in the main of the work done in the *Philosophical Commentaries*. The "ingenious friends" who helped in the revision included Matthew French and Samuel Madden, both of them scholars and men of distinction in later life (see PC, no. 569), Sir John and Lady Percival, and Samuel Molyneux, distinguished son of the distinguished William Molyneux, whom Locke was proud to call his friend.*

Samuel Molyneux was Berkeley's confidant in philosophical matters, and Berkeley's recently discovered letters to him (Nos. 1, 4, 5 and 6)† show the two friends discussing *inter alia* Berkeley's own philosophy. Letter No. 5 has an interesting postscript which tells of a senior colleague seeing the manuscript of the *Principles* before publication and advising on it:

"I have lately had much Talk with Dr. Elwood‡ about my Notion, I have communicated my Design & papers to him & am glad I have done so, for I find he is a Man of very good sense."

* Locke's *Essay*, II, ix, 8.   † *Works*, Vol. VIII.

‡ John Elwood, Jurist Fellow, was elected to fellowship in 1696. As a lawyer he was exempted from the celibacy statute and from the obligation to take Holy Orders. He became Vice-Provost and Member of Parliament for the University. He died in 1740, leaving a legacy of £1,000 to the College.

In his reply to the second charge Berkeley placed his finger on the main motive of the revision and the driving force behind it, viz. the fear of being confounded with the sceptics. The fear can be illustrated from entry after entry in the *Commentaries*; and when he was making those entries, his fear was not only that of being confounded with the sceptics, but of actually *being* a sceptic; and it was a well-grounded fear in those days; he had been to the edge of the precipice and looked over; that may be why he took this criticism so hard; it *had* been true of him, or nearly so. French immaterialism contained the seeds of French scepticism as Bayle proved to the hilt. But *now* the thesis has been revised; *now* the *Principles* is published, and now the author says with truth that there is a direct opposition between his principles and those of the sceptics; he says now with truth, "I question not the existence of anything that we perceive by our senses." That is the very hinge of his *revised* immaterialism. He could not have made that statement with truth two or three years earlier; it was not true of his "first arguings". In earlier days he did doubt, if not deny, the existence of sensible things; and at times, as we shall see, he had felt so confused about personality, that he hardly knew whether he himself existed or not.

CHAPTER II

BERKELEY'S DIALECTICAL METHOD

READERS of Berkeley's books should know something of their background, and something of his method of exposition. They should know that Berkeley spent five or six years on preparatory work for the *Principles*, and yet that "gross misinterpretation" of some passages in it is on first reading unavoidable. They should know that the work in draft was carefully examined and revised by the author, and was radically altered by him after an intellectual conversion. They should know that his first argument for immaterialism relied on a panpsychist metaphysic, which he gradually abandoned during the course of the revision, and that his second thoughts about it were based on (what he took to be) a common-sense principle. They should know that a large number of entries in the revision notebooks represent his discarded views, distinguished by the marginal sign "+". Finally they should know that Berkeley was at one time sceptical about the existence of the world of sense, but had renounced his scepticism two years or more before the *Principles* was published, and solemnly declared before God shortly after its publication, and about its contents, "I question not the existence of anything that we perceive by our senses."

Background and discarded views and method of exposition may seem to some readers of minor importance compared with the actual teaching. Why not read the *Principles*, and find out for ourselves what Berkeley does teach? That is where the shoe pinches. Without some background knowledge, without some acquaintance with the views discarded, without some appreciation of Berkeley's method of exposition, it is very hard to find out exactly what he does teach. People have been reading the *Principles* for two hundred and fifty years, and important points about it are still in dispute; and some of our disputes are due to neglect of that background and that method to which Berkeley called attention.

Berkeley's teaching is not all on the surface, and it is conditioned by the reader's learning. In a sense he teaches different things to different people; for he teaches as the reader is able to hear and receive it. The question is not so much what the *Principles* teaches, as what we can learn from its teaching. Berkeley once wrote to his friend, Samuel Johnson:

> "I do not therefore pretend that my books can teach truth. All I hope for is, that they may be an occasion to inquisitive men of discovering truth, by consulting their own minds, and looking into their own thoughts."*

The words are the utterance of modesty and of method. Taken along with other passages in his writings they suggest that there was an element in Berkeley's development that can be called dialectical, and that this element is reflected in the structure of the *Principles* and in the method of his exposition.

I am not using the term *dialectical* in a very precise sense. Berkeley's dialectic is not the Platonic dialectic, "the coping-stone of the sciences"† nor Hegel's triadic movement of abstract thought; yet there is something of Plato and of Hegel in the *Commentaries* and the *Principles*. There is learning by question and answer and by trial and error; knowledge is acquired by partial truths that verge on error, and are taken up as moments into a higher truth; and there is a sense of inner compulsion, of following the argument whithersoever it leads, of a movement of thought according to plan, transcending personal thinking.

Berkeley filling his notebooks in his "wonder year" is the perfect example of the "inquisitive" man, all set to discover truth by consulting his own mind and looking into his own thoughts. He proceeded by question and answer, more questions, more answers, mistakes, corrections of mistakes, and corrections of corrections. The argument led him a long, hard

* Berkeley to Johnson, *Works*, Vol. II, p. 282.
† *Republic*, Book VII, 534 E.

and roundabout way; but he followed it. His revised immaterialism took shape in his mind and on paper, as we shall see, gradually after a long process of trial and error. Not only did he profit by his mistakes, but his errors were an essential part of his doctrinal development, and I think he expected a similar development in his readers; they are to reach his standpoint by sharing his experience rather perhaps than by imbibing his teaching. Looking back on his apprenticeship Berkeley was aware of intellectual currents curbing, controlling and bearing him along. He had learned through half-truths and transient errors. His second thoughts on matter were his first arguings sublimated; and a sublimation is "a solid substance deposited as a result of a cooling of vapours". In the cooling of Berkeley's vapours dialectic played a decisive part.

In ancient Greece dialectic was the method of seeking truth by disciplined conversation and ordered discourse as distinct from formal instruction and set speeches. The dialectician asked questions and questioned the answers. The entries in Berkeley's notebooks are almost entirely conversational. Scores of them have the formal "Qu:" prefixed; scores more ask questions directly or indirectly. Berkeley is questioning his other self. Berkeley *major* is holding a seminar, so to speak, with Berkeley *minor*. Hence the tension in the notebooks, and the bi-polarity of the thought. Hence the shifting standpoints, the oscillation and the quick movements to and fro, like that of the shuttle in the loom, as the thinker weaves his reasoned web out of partial, mistaken and conflicting views. Such was the dialectic in the Socratic circle in the streets of Athens long ago, in the classrooms of the Academy and in the earlier dialogues of Plato, when a deep problem was thrashed out by probing questions and provocative answers, and thought rose towards truth on stepping-stones of mistaken and discarded thoughts.

By way of illustration here is a crucial piece of Berkeley's dialectic. I have put it together from actual entries that run from near the beginning of the *Commentaries* to the end. He is wrestling with the problem of body. Picture him in his College rooms, seated at the table with his notebook open before him. He is looking out on the College park, and every now and then glancing up at the Dublin mountains. He meditates and writes, writes and meditates:

"If there is no matter, then nothing exists but mind. I can be sure of nothing but God and finite spirits. There is no body. What then are these chairs and tables, and the trees out there and the mountains? They look solid enough; but they cannot really exist; for they have no material substance, and they are not minds or souls. After all I see things like them in dreams, which prove to be flimsy and transient, moving in and out of existence with the wanderings of the dream. The sceptics are right; there is no external world of bodies; at least we cannot be sure of it.

"But that won't do. Scepticism is a slippery slope. If I cannot be sure of God's world, how can I be sure of God? Or for that matter, how can I be sure of my own existence? Chairs and tables, trees and mountains are not material things; they do not exist in material substance; but they must exist somehow, somewhere. But how and where?

"Locke explained appearance by powers; could I do the same? Locke made secondary qualities nothing but powers in body to produce ideas in us. That's it. Bodies are powers in God, or combinations of powers in God, to make us perceive. In that sense they exist. That saves the phenomena without recourse to matter.

"But does it? Can a body *be* a power or a combination of powers in God? Power is a compound idea; it involves the causal relation. God causing an effect *in God*? That can't be right. That's pantheism. Then the term *body* must have two meanings. Bodies must be combinations of thoughts, and combinations of powers to raise thoughts. But those two meanings are incompatible. They could not combine in God, any more than in thought. I will keep the former and drop the latter. I will not mention the combinations of powers.

I will say the things themselves really exist, the effects of God's powers."

The above is a free rendering of the "combinations of powers" debate, which is analysed in detail below (p. 133). When we consider it along with other well-defined trains of thought in the *Commentaries*, all pointing in the one direction, we realize what a momentous change the revision involved, and how rapid and revolutionary Berkeley's doctrinal development was when he was filling these notebooks. He began the year a panpsychist; he ended it a panentheist; he began with a bodiless world of spirits; he ended with a world of spirit and sensible body.

With this fact before us we can appreciate Berkeley's method of exposition and see its significance. Berkeley could not forget the dialectical value of his own past errors. "Chairs and tables are combinations of powers in God." The challenging remark proved to be an error, but it was provocative of thought. Once it was made, the dialectical discussion it provoked had to go on till the truth about it was found. Looking back on the period Berkeley saw that the time he had spent in error was time spent in finding truth. If he had not thought that chairs and tables were mental entities that go in and out of existence according as we think of them and cease to think of them, he would never have advanced to his final conception of an independent world of continuing sensible things, grounded in the universal Mind. If he had not been a panpsychist for a year or two, he might never have become a panentheist. The method of learning truth through temporary error pervades the *Commentaries*, and it accounts for a good deal in the planning of the *Principles*.

Berkeley recognized, too, the involuntary element in philosophical thought. The most striking instance is the passage, quoted above (p. 17) from the conclusion of the third Dialogue. In the spirit of Heraclitus who said "the way up and the way down are one and the same", Berkeley wrote that the ascent of the round column of water and its descent proceed "from the same uniform law or principle of *gravitation*. Just so, the same principles which at first view lead to *scepticism*, pursued to a certain point, bring men back to common sense." Berkeley is speaking from experience; he is telling the inner story of his own early development. He had to reason and speculate. With the Academics and Cartesians he had to question the evidence of sense and the existence of the world of sense. He had to rise with the sublime notions of Malebranche, and then sink back again to earth, to the dictates of nature and common sense. It was the logical pattern of events; it all had to be.

Berkeley expected misunderstanding and misinterpretation of his teaching; he expected a time-lag between first acquaintance with the *Principles* and a full understanding of it. In the Preface he begs the reader to suspend judgment on the merits of the book till he has read the whole through attentively at least once, saying "there are some passages that, taken by themselves, are very liable (nor could it be remedied) to gross misinterpretation, and to be charged with most absurd consequences, which, nevertheless, upon an entire perusal will appear not to follow from them". This is a remarkable admission for any author to make. He had revised the work after a long and scrupulous inquiry, and yet he is bound to be misunderstood; he does not lay it at the reader's door; it is not negligence or haste on the part of the reader; it is something in the situation; the difficulties of expounding immaterialism are so great that Berkeley has had to practise an economy of truth, and say things that cannot be rightly understood on first reading. Such passages must be misunderstood in order to be understood eventually.

Let us consider the first and chiefest of these passages, viz. section 1 in the body of the work. Taken by itself it is very liable to gross misinterpretation, and to be charged with most absurd consequences. The key words in it are, "Other collections of ideas constitute a stone, a tree, a book, and the like sensible things." Berkeley has prepared the way for this statement adroitly; the familiar Lockeian phrase "ideas of light and colours" acts as a shock-absorber; and the reader does not take in at first what has been said; he thinks Berkeley is talking only about ideas of stones, trees, books etc. But that is not so. Berkeley is not talking about ideas of stones, trees, and books. He is talking about ideas that *are* stones, trees and books. He says that collections of ideas *constitute* these and the like sensible things. Not till we linger on the words do we taste their full flavour, their full meaning and their full absurdity. Fancy throwing a stone made up of ideas. Fancy planting an apple-tree, made up of ideas, and expecting it to grow and produce apples.

Why did not Berkeley forestall and obviate this line of criticism? A sentence or two in the Introduction, explaining that he was using the term *idea* in a specialist sense, would have done it; he had only to say that *idea* was the only available term of precision for the immediate object of sense, and was not a mental entity. He did none of these things. Instead, he almost courted misinterpretation, and invited the charge of absurdity. What he states, read in the light of the whole work, is perfectly correct; he does not overstate or understate his case; there is not a word in section 1 inconsistent with his full and final doctrine; but he has not taken steps in it to avoid this grave misconstruction; it looks as if he had deliberately chosen to give the impression that sensible things are mental in order to drive home the lesson of their dependence upon mind, and place their mind-reference beyond dispute.

He soon began to correct this first impression, but he was in no hurry to complete the process. In section 2 he laid down that the mind is "a thing entirely distinct" from ideas, and in section 25 he began to stress the passivity of ideas and the activity of mind. In section 49 he virtually denied that sensible things are modes or attributes of mind, and in section 89 he stated that spirits and ideas are "two kinds, entirely distinct and heterogeneous". Finally, when all objections were answered and his argument complete, he produced (section 144) the key term "sensible ideas", instancing a ball in motion and the stroke of a racket. Berkeley had long had the term *sensible idea* in mind; he used it in the *Commentaries* (Nos. 478, 544); but whether by accident or design he did not use it in the *Principles* till the end. A *sensible idea* is an idea that can be sensed, seen or touched. It clinches Berkeley's account of the external world, and proves that he did not intend his ideas of sense to be permanently regarded as mental entities; his expressed intention was to turn ideas into things without turning things into ideas.* A Hegelian might call Berkeley's *sensible idea* the truth of his idea of sense; and certainly the phrase "sensible ideas" in section 144 neatly rounds off the silent dialectic that began in section 1 with the phrase "collections of ideas".

"Nor could it be remedied," says the Preface about the liability to misrepresentation and the charge of absurdity. Why not? Why could it not be remedied? Partial views mislead, and passages torn from their context may sound absurd and be absurd. All authors know it, and guard against it. Berkeley was a resourceful writer; why could he not have found a remedy by correcting the accent and emphasis, and a timely use of illustration? He could find no remedy, he says. The authorship is not at fault. The *Principles* is well planned; the language is simple, and the meaning of most sentences is quite clear. Yet we have only to recall our own first acquaintance with the book to endorse Berkeley's judgment. Parts of it are liable to gross misinterpretation and are chargeable with most absurd consequences. The meaning of key phrases such as "in the mind" is folded up in many wrappings like a child's Christmas present. Berkeley's teaching, though in itself simple, runs counter to the received opinion of two thousand years; it is therefore complex and subtle in the learning, and much has to be left to time and the reader's intellectual development. Immaterialism has to be assimilated piecemeal, not swallowed holus-bolus. Berkeley himself misinterpreted it grossly at first, and took the best part of three years to straighten things out.

* *Works*, Vol. II, p. 244.

Look at the yellowing pages of his notebooks; he learned his revised immaterialism there literally "line upon line, line upon line, here a little and there a little". We must learn, as he learned. The dangers and pitfalls are still there; and there is no remedy except patient learning and an appreciation of his method.

Let me illustrate it again. While Berkeley held that chairs and tables were powers in God, he had to hold, and did hold, that they were intermittent existents; for a power is an activity, exerted intermittently. He had to hold, and did hold, that the chairs and tables in his study went in and out of existence, like the chairs and tables of a dream. Along with intermittency go annihilation and perpetual re-creation; for the intermittent object melts into nothingness, and is re-born as if created anew. The trio of doctrines can be clearly traced through the notebooks, and I give the evidence below (p. 133). Berkeley dropped the theory, when he re-found his common-sense belief in body; but the theory makes an ambiguous appearance, that might be called *dialectical*, in sections 45–8 of the *Principles*.

We will study those four sections; they form a fine illustration of Berkeley's method. But first let me say that I regard the intermittency theory as little short of absurd. The prose of life requires stability and relative permanence in the things of sense. Only a fool would prepare to sit down on a chair that was not yet there. Only a madman would drive at speed round the bend of a road-to-be. By this issue, therefore, Berkeley's claim to have renounced paradox, and to have returned to common sense, may fairly be judged. But I have to appear as a sort of "devil's advocate" for intermittency. I have to justify Berkeley's tender treatment of it, though my instinct (and, I dare say, that of my readers) is to give it short shrift. We need to put a brake on our natural impatience with this trio of doctrines. Berkeley was patient with them, even when he no longer believed in them; and I think he drew his patience from considering the intermittency of the creative imagination. He asks:

G.   *Why may we not conceive it possible for God to create*
        things out of Nothing. certainly we our selves create in
        some wise whenever we imagine.

                                                        (No. 830)

Shakespeare says:

>   These our actors,
>   As I foretold you, were all spirits, and
>   Are melted into air, into thin air:
>   And, like the baseless fabric of this vision,
>   The cloud-capp'd towers, the gorgeous palaces,
>   The solemn temples, the great globe itself,
>   Yea, all which it inherit, shall dissolve,
>   And, like this insubstantial pageant faded,
>   Leave not a wrack behind.*

Prospero is thinking of the end of his "rough magic", of his
actors melting into thin air and the annihilation of his insub-
stantial pageant. But readers who in any degree know the
power of the drama and the magic of the spoken word, will
think too of the day when Shakespeare summoned the en-
chanted island from the vasty deep, and said, Let Ariel be, and
Prospero and Miranda and Ferdinand and Caliban. What is
not *was* till the scene was done and the curtain fell; and the
round continued—creation, intermittent existence, annihilation—till the play was done.

The imagination is one faculty, and sense-perception is
another; but the two faculties somehow live and grow together
in one embodied mind. As philosophers our first business is
with the perception of the world and the supposed intermittency of the percept; and the issue here is the touchstone of a
sane interpretation of Berkeley's philosophy. We are trying to
determine what Berkeley actually teaches in the *Principles* about
the world perceived, and how he came to teach it. We find from
his notebooks that in 1707 he believed in intermittency and the
companion doctrines, and that a year later he had given them

* *The Tempest*, IV, 1.

C

up. He knew it was a crux, and he devoted four sections in the *Principles* to the issue; but in those sections he showed himself so sympathetic towards the discarded doctrines that he must have meant his readers to share that sympathy for a while.

I suggest that the creative imagination is the psychological key; in view of the facts of artistic creation and the temporarily real status of the objects thus created, it is impossible for a philosopher to treat the intermittency doctrines as absurd; and that is why, I think, Berkeley handles the issue as he does. He had rejected the doctrines, but he treats them as useful propaedeutics, not to be lightly brushed aside. He decides definitely against them, but delays his verdict till the very end.

The sections* to be considered open vividly:

> "Fourthly, it will be objected that from the foregoing principles it follows, things are every moment annihilated and created anew. The objects of sense exist only when they are perceived: the trees therefore are in the garden, or the chairs in the parlour, no longer than while there is some body by to perceive them. Upon shutting my eyes all the furniture in the room is reduced to nothing, and barely upon opening them it is again created."

This objection, the fourth of the series, is forcibly expressed. Berkeley has put it so graphically and with such point that readers often take it as an expression of Berkeley's own opinion, and not an objection he proposes to answer. It is in fact a bit of both. That the objects of sense exist only when they are perceived Berkeley believed; that things are every moment annihilated and created anew he did not believe. He believed there is always somebody by to perceive them; that when I shut my eyes all the furniture in the room is reduced to nothing he did not believe. However, for his own reasons Berkeley has not distinguished part from part; but has treated the objection as a whole, and has gone out of his way to defend it up to a point. The absurdities in question, charged against his doctrine, are,

* *Principles*, 45–8.

he says, "pretended absurdities"; in other words they are not
absurdities at all. We are to hold, it would seem, that there is
nothing absurd in vanishing furniture, in chairs that melt into
thin air, like Ariel, and in tables that go in and out of existence,
like the Cheshire cat.

In the next two sections (46, 47) Berkeley comes to the same
point from a different angle. He meets the Objector with a
tu quoque. It may be thought absurd that upon closing my eyes
all the visible objects around me should be annihilated; but
that is exactly what is taught by contemporary philosophers
and accepted by contemporary thinkers. Locke, for instance,
teaches that light and colours are mere sensations which exist
only while they are perceived, and are annihilated when they
cease to be perceived.

Then there is the difficulty about continual creation. Some
think the doctrine absurd; yet it is commonly taught in the
Schools. The Scholastics say that the material substance of the
fabric of the external world is maintained by divine conservation, which they explain as a continual creation. If responsible,
trained philosophers can hold and teach the continual creation
of material substance, why boggle at the continual creation of
chairs and tables?

Berkeley then turns to the materialists. He has the mathematicians chiefly in mind; for he concentrates on the supposed
infinite divisibility of matter; but his argument applies equally
to all materialist theories of perception. If the existence of
matter be granted, he argues, we are bound to hold the intermittent existence of the particular bodies perceived by sense;
for neither they, nor anything like them, can on that theory
exist when they are no longer perceived.

Thus in three consecutive sections (45, 46, 47) Berkeley has
defended our trio of doctrines from the charge of absurdity.
Then, and not till then, does he show his hand. These tenets are
not absurd; but he does not hold them. In section 48 he says
again that objects of sense are "nothing else but ideas". The
phrase means just what it says, and is not depreciatory. The

objects of sense, being ideas, have no second or material existence. Being ideas, they cannot exist unperceived; but we are
not entitled to infer that they have only an intermittent existence, ceasing to be when men cease to perceive them. There
may be some other spirit that perceives them though we do not.
They cannot exist *without the mind*; but that phrase is not to be
taken of this or that particular mind, but of all minds whatsoever. Then comes the decisive declaration to which all four
sections point: "It does not therefore follow from the foregoing
principles, that bodies are annihilated and created every
moment, or exist not at all during the intervals between our
perception of them."

It is a clear and unambiguous conclusion, which goes to the
heart of Berkeleian interpretation. In view of it no consistent
Berkeleian can hold that chairs and tables go in and out o
existence according as they are perceived by man or not. The
conclusion has been reached in a circuitous manner that calls
for explanation. Berkeley has argued effectively that intermittency with its two companion doctrines, commonly thought
absurd, are not absurd. He himself had held them to be true for
two years or more, and he had not found them absurd; they
had not satisfied him, but they had made him think beyond his
own mind; they had made him think philosophically of "all
minds whatsoever". They had not satisfied him; he does not
hold them to be true now; he has dissociated the doctrine of the
Principles from them; he has said categorically that they do not
follow from his principles; but he took a long time to say so;
and it is clear that he himself had derived benefit from them,
and thought that his readers might do the same.

Intermittency is stated or assumed in the earlier entries in the
notebooks; but as the conception of real, immaterial body took
shape in Berkeley's mind, intermittency and the companion
doctrines passed out. In the summer and autumn of 1707 he
officially believed that chairs and tables ceased to be when we
ceased to see and touch them, and were created anew as our
need for them arose. How far he carried the belief, I do not

know, nor how he squared it with practice. Intermittency, annihilation and perpetual re-creation were paradoxes that followed, Berkeley thought, from the sublime notions of immaterialism he then held. A year later, say by the summer of 1708, all that was changed; the revolt, revulsion and conversion had taken place; and the revision was nearly complete. Common sense and the fear of scepticism had won the day. Berkeley no longer accepted the triple paradox.

How then will he treat the three doctrines when he has to deal with them officially in the *Principles*? He will treat them as an objection to be answered. He will put them into the mouth of an objector as a trio of absurdities chargeable against immaterialism. So far, so good; for many men think of matter as the permanent reality in the background, which throws transient pictures of itself on the screen of sense-perception; and to rob them of matter (as Berkeley is doing, they think) is to rob them of reality. The objection must be answered. How then will Berkeley answer it?

Will he give intermittency short shrift? Will he round on this trio of doctrines with the zeal of a new convert to common sense? Will he condemn them root and branch, call them nonsense, and warn his readers against them? No. He was too wise, too conscious of their dialectical value, too grateful for what he himself owed to them. Instead of attacking them he defended them from the charge of absurdity. He commended them to the notice and attention of his readers, and declared that responsible thinkers, past and present, held views like them. He wished these views to be examined and entertained; and on the top of all that he declared categorically that these views do not follow from his principles.

Thus in his *Principles* Berkeley has given a practical example of his dialectical method. His teaching on intermittency, existence in the mind and sensible ideas constitutes a dialectical immaterialism, in which the part cries out for the whole. Luminous paradoxes, useful falsities and self-refuting half-truths had all formed part of Berkeley's experience during the preparatory work of the *Principles*; they had helped him and had failed him; they were all part of the upward and downward path; they had to be. Berkeley shares his experience with his *full-time* readers; and when in the Preface he gave warning of inevitable mistakes and misinterpretations, said there was no remedy, and appealed for "entire perusal", he meant, I think, that only by entertaining for a time wrong and inadequate notions of immaterialism, and passing beyond them, can his readers be weaned from the ancient and ingrained notions of material substance and absolute existence, and learn to interpret permanence, stability and reality in terms of mind and spirit.

CHAPTER III

BERKELEY'S EARLY WRITINGS

BERKELEY originally undertook his study of immaterialism, I believe, as a research thesis, designed to promote his chances of winning a Fellowship. Had it been a purely disinterested speculation, he could hardly have afforded to devote so much time and attention to it; for he had his career to make, and he was not a wealthy man. For five post-graduate years the immaterial hypothesis was the focus of his intellectual life and writings, and during the first three of those years the Fellowship examination hung over his head like a sword of Damocles.

In the spring of 1704 at the age of nineteen Berkeley took the degree of Bachelor of Arts at the University of Dublin, which then, as now, was closely identified with Trinity College. His father, William Berkeley, of Thomastown, was a gentleman farmer with a revenue appointment. He had six sons and at least one daughter. He appears as "generosus" in the matriculation book, when George, the eldest child, entered College in 1700. He had military rank (*"vexill. equestris"*) when a younger son, Robert, matriculated in 1717. He served as Cornet of Dragoons under the Earl of Galway, and was taken prisoner at the battle of Almanzar.* He gave three of his sons a university education; he was probably not in a position to do much more for them.

As an undergraduate George had distinguished himself in classics, mathematics and philosophy, and he was obviously cut out for academic life. The only way he could enter it was by being elected a Fellow, and the only road to a Fellowship was through an open competitive examination on advanced courses; but the electors would naturally be impressed by merit

---

* Almanzar was fought 25 April 1707—the eve of Berkeley's Fellowship examination.

shown in a published thesis. The lot of a Fellowship-candidate was not a happy one. Elections were held only when vacancies occurred, and a candidate might wait for years, not knowing when the next election would be.

Berkeley had to wait three years in the wilderness; during that *triennium* he did the spade-work of his thesis on immaterialism, and wrote the essay or group of essays that he called "my first arguings". This stage came to an end in the autumn of 1706, when William Mullart* resigned his Fellowship, and an election to fill the vacancy was announced for the following June. Berkeley's chance had come, and he seized it with both hands. Laying aside his work on immaterialism which was not ready for the press, he ransacked his desk, found some mathematical trifles, written two or three years earlier, worked them up into the form of a book, wrote elegant Latin dedications and a Preface, and published it anonymously under the titles *Arithmetica* and *Miscellanea Mathematica*, with profuse apologies for the triviality of its contents, with several references to his other reading and writing, and with a promise of better things.†
The book has some slight local interest; it would prove to the electors that the author could write good Latin, but as a contribution to knowledge it is almost negligible. On 9 June 1707 Berkeley was elected a Fellow "having previously sustained with honour the very trying examination which the candidates for that preferment are by the statutes required to undergo".‡

Election to his Fellowship made little immediate difference to his way of life. He continued to live on in the College, reading widely, thinking and writing much. His mind was now

---

* Ten years earlier Mullart had been in Berkeley's position, a Fellowship-candidate, and was employed by Molyneux to translate Locke's *Essay* into Latin. He had made considerable progress in that monumental task when a Fellowship fell vacant; then he had to suspend his translating and concentrate on the examination. See *Some Familiar Letters between Mr. Locke and Several of His Friends* (London, 1700), pp. 112, 122.

† See *Works*, Vol. IV, pp. 168, 206, 214, 220, 221.

‡ J. Stock, *Life of Berkeley*.

at rest about his career, and he was assured of a modest competence in congenial surroundings. A little light lecturing came
his way, and a few extra calls upon his time; but not until he
was appointed Librarian in November 1709 was he seriously
involved in the administrative machine; and by that time the
manuscript of the *Principles* was completed and ready for the
press.

Against that background Berkeley's early writings are seen
in true perspective. Their author was not a youthful prodigy
with a freakish mind who somehow tumbled into academic life,
and for no apparent reason started to write great books.
Before he was twenty-six years old he had written and published three books, two of them philosophical classics. He was
exceptionally talented, and his environment was exceptionally
favourable. During his creative period, the *quinquennium* 1704–9,
he lived among books and the learned with few distractions. He
lived at a time of intellectual ferment, when the old philosophy
was passing, when new philosophies were in the air and a man
was free to think for himself. He had leisure and a competence,
a library at hand, and opportunities for research. He had the
motive—a career to make; last, but not least, he had chanced on
the perfect theme for a Fellowship thesis, congenial, challenging,
well-defined and in line with his personal interests. Does matter
exist? The question involved wide reading on the chief subjects
of the Fellowship examination. Philosophy and mathematics,
physics, optics and dioptrics—he must keep up with them all in
order to cope with the problem of matter. He must read the
writings of Descartes, Leibniz and Spinoza, of Locke and
Malebranche, of Newton, Keill, Barrow and Molyneux. Immaterialism was the ideal theme for him; he could pursue at
one and the same time truth, knowledge, fame and his bread
and butter.

Berkeley first met his problem when he first met the writings
of Malebranche, and that was, almost certainly, in his undergraduate days. Malebranche by then was well known in Eng-
land. Norris and Collier owed much to him. Locke wrote

against him. Men of letters referred to him. He was well known, too, to the intelligentsia of Dublin, to Palliser and the Molyneux family and others in Berkeley's immediate circle. Berkeley first mentions Malebranche in his *De ludo algebraico*, which was written probably in 1704–5. He speaks there as if he knew the whole of the *Recherche*, and had practised Malebranche's Rules of Method.* He probably started work on the "immaterial hypothesis", as he called it, soon after taking his B.A. degree in 1704. If so, he would have had nearly two and a half years to work out its ramifications before Mullart's Fellowship fell vacant in the autumn of 1706. When that occurred, the thesis had to be set aside. Like Mullart himself ten years earlier, Berkeley had to concentrate on the examination; he was, as he says, "*aliis studiis occupato*".† When the examination and election were successfully over, Berkeley came back to his thesis. Perhaps he came back sobered by the six months' interruption. To write a student's academic thesis on the views of a French monk was one thing; to publish his own views on the external world was another thing. He was now a responsible member of the University staff, shortly to take Holy Orders, and he had looked French scepticism in the face. Dare he publish a book denying the existence of matter, if that meant denying the existence of the world of sense? With such thoughts in mind, it would seem, the new Fellow of his College came back to his immaterial hypothesis in July or August 1707, and began to examine, reconsider and revise his previous work.

I will now give a complete list, for the convenience of students, of Berkeley's writings of the early period, so far as we have them, or know of them. I have not included the letters; they may be seen in Volume VIII of the *Works*, pp. 19–33. The items are in chronological order, and I give explanatory comments on those that bear on the development of Berkeley's thought and his revision of his thesis. The list closes with the publication of the *Principles*. All are extant except No. 3.

* *Works*, Vol. IV, pp. 219–20.
† ib., p. 214.

LIST OF BERKELEY'S EARLY WRITINGS

(1) A Description of the Cave of Dunmore, *c.* 1706; *Works*, Vol. IV, p. 257.

(2) Communication to Hans Sloane, 11 June 1706; *Works*, Vol. IX, p. 161.

(3) "My first arguings", *c.* 1704 to *c.* September 1706.

(4) *Arithmetica* and *Miscellanea Mathematica*, London, 1707; *Works*, Vol. IV, p. 165.

(5) Philosophical Commentaries, notebook B,* *c.* July, 1707 to *c.* December 1707; *Works*, Vol. I, p. 9.

(6) "Of Infinites", November 1707; *Works*, Vol. IV, p. 235.

(7) Philosophical Commentaries, notebook A, *c.* December 1707 to August 1708; *Works*, Vol. I, p. 50.

(8) Sermon, On Immortality, 11 January 1708; *Works*, Vol. VII, p. 9.

(9) Draft Introduction to the *Principles*, 15 November 1708 to 18 December 1708; *Works*, Vol. II, p. 121.

(10) *An Essay towards a New Theory of Vision*, Dublin, *c.* July, 1709; second edition 1709–10; *Works*, Vol. I, p. 171.

(11) Draft of the *Principles*, sections 85–145. British Museum, Add. MS. 39304, ff. 35–105.

(12) *A Treatise concerning the Principles of Human Knowledge*, Dublin, May 1710.

In the above list Nos. 3, 5 and 7 are of outstanding importance for our purpose, and they are discussed at length later in this chapter; but first a few remarks on some of the other items must be made.

Berkeley's Description of the Cave of Dunmore (No. 1) and his Communication (No. 2), recently identified as Berkeley's, to Hans Sloane, Irish-born Secretary of the Royal Society, are of no philosophical importance except as evidence of his keen interest in physical phenomena and the external world.

Berkeley's first publication (No. 4) with its double title, two

* The terms "notebook B" and "notebook A" are explained below, p. 55.

title-pages, two dedications, one Preface and continuous pagina-
tion, bears every mark of hasty construction. I have already
commented on the triviality of its contents. It is hard to believe
that he had any such publication in view when he first put his
hand to the plough of authorship. His original intention was,
I believe, to put out a monograph on immaterialism; but either
his theme proved intractable, or the Fellowship fell vacant sooner
than was expected; the thesis was not ready for publication,
and he set it aside for further thought and ultimate revision.
Then he decided on an *interim* publication, raked together these
juvenilia, and made a presentable booklet of them.

His short tract "Of Infinites" (No. 6) is an integral part of
the case for immaterialism; for if infinitely divisible real parts
existed, they would be imperceptible realities, and the *esse est
percipi* would fail. Berkeley here takes up Locke's distinction*
between the idea of the infinity of space and the idea of space
infinite, and uses it to show that the fact that we can go on
dividing a space in thought indefinitely does not imply that a
finite space can actually be divided into an infinite number of
real parts.

Two autograph copies of the tract exist, the one in the library
of Trinity College, Dublin, the other in the Sloane Papers
(Add. MS. 4812, f. 14) in the British Museum. The former copy
has long been known as Berkeley's; it bears no date, and Fraser
mistakenly dated it "1705 or 1706". The latter copy was
identified as Berkeley's only the other day (its "G.B." had been
interpreted as "George Brown", instead of "George Berkeley").
The heading states that it was read before the Dublin Society
on 19 November 1707. The discovery of this precise date has
enabled me to assign the approximate dates, shown on the
above List, for the conclusion of notebook B and the beginning
of notebook A; for a duplicated series of entries, connected
with the tract, appears towards the end of notebook B (Nos.
351–8) and near the beginning of notebook A (Nos. 415, 416,
420–4).

* *Essay*, II, xvii, 7.

The Draft Introduction* to the *Principles* (No. 9) is substantially the same as the published Introduction. It was a consequence of the revision; for as originally planned the Introduction was to have been on simple ideas and demonstration. The
theme, abstract general ideas, came to Berkeley while he was
filling the latter part of notebook B, and the attack on abstraction was fully mounted at the outset of notebook A.† The Draft
Introduction is evidence of Berkeley's methodical habits and
attention to detail. Quotations are written out in full in the
italic hand, and every paragraph is dated to a day. Berkeley
wrote a short piece of it almost every day from 15 November
1708 to 18 December 1708. A large number of pages have been
cut out of the notebook, leaving the stubs, after the Introduction. Presumably the notebook originally contained a draft of
the body of the work or the first part of it. Berkeley's notebooks
must have been beside him on the table when he wrote the
Draft Introduction, for several entries about it which did not
reach the printed Introduction appear in the Draft, viz. Nos.
566, 588, 592, 600, 607, 648, 727, 727a and 737.

The Draft of the *Principles*, sections 85–145 (No. 11) is curiously placed in its notebook. Berkeley began the draft a third of
the way through a new notebook, leaving over fifty folios blank.
Clearly he intended to use them for a draft of the first half of the
Principles. Has this gap anything to do, one wonders, with the
pages cut from the Chapman Manuscript? The differences between the text of the draft and the text of the first and second
editions are noted in Professor Jessop's apparatus in Volume II
of the *Works*. Jessop writes, "The most interesting result of this
collation is that when Berkeley introduced the term *notion* in a
restricted sense in his second edition he did but restore what he
had originally intended to include in the first (see note to
section 140). The term only, not the doctrine it indicated, was

* Its *prima manu* text is printed in *Works*, Vol. II, pp. 121–45. The
autograph is in the notebook, known as "the Chapman manuscript" (D 5 17,
ff. 1–33) in the library of Trinity College, Dublin.

† See below (p. 109) and PC, Nos. 212, 318, 401.

omitted from the first edition."* The draft has incorporated the main results of the doctrinal revision of 1707–8 and of the discussions in the *Commentaries*. It is very like the published work both in phrase and doctrine, and was probably the final draft before the copy was sent to the press.

The rest of this chapter constitutes a literary introduction to those early writings (Nos. 3, 5, 7) by Berkeley on which the present work centres. I have to write at length and in detail, because much of the information, here given, is new, or not generally known, and is essential to a clear understanding of the making of the *Principles*. It is just because the two notebooks have survived in which Berkeley commented on his previous writings on immaterialism, and revised them, that we know how and by what steps the *Principles* came to be.

The first arguings (No. 3), as such, are not extant. The term is comprehensive and can cover argument written and unwritten. I do not wish to narrow its meaning unduly or to tie it down too precisely, but I use it (as I believe Berkeley did) to cover his writings on immaterialism *before* his intensive preparation for the Fellowship examination. Berkeley uses the term in the following entry:

MP   *ffrom Malbranch, Locke & my first arguings it cant be prov'd that extension is not in matter ffrom Lockes arguings it can't be prov'd that Colours are not in Bodies.*
                                                                    (No. 265)

This entry marks a turning-point in the revision. Berkeley is on the point of discovering his "new principle", viz. *esse est percipi*; and he here expresses dissatisfaction with his old principle. A change of method and a re-start are in view. Berkeley refers to the change in sections 14 and 15 of the *Principles*, where he contrasts the method of arguing pursued by modern philosophers with his own method, viz. "the arguments foregoing". *They*

* T. E. Jessop, *The first edition of the Principles*, 1937, Preface. I have made a detailed survey of the texts of the Draft and the published work (sections 85–145) and have given the results below in Appendix III.

argue from the relativity of the secondary qualities, and their dependence on mind; but that argument even when it is widened to take in the primary qualities, Berkeley says, does not prove that there is no extension or colour in an outward object, but only that we do not know by sense which is its true extension or colour. On the other hand his own argument from the nature of existence, he claims, plainly shows that there is no such thing as an outward object.

The modern philosophers in view are Locke and Malebranche. Berkeley names them in the entry under discussion, and uses their names as synonyms for their writings; he juxtaposes *Locke*, *Malbranch* and *my first arguings*, and immediately goes on to speak of *Locke's arguings*, and it is a very strong presumption that "my first arguings" were written, too. Besides, this entry represents a doctrinal decision taken after two or three years of thought. The arguings concerned had already reached such dimensions that no one could possibly carry them all in his head. Written work is assumed by the entries dealing with time and vision (as I show below), and is almost certainly referred to in No. 69 ("Wt I have said . . ."), in No. 209 ("to correct my language") and in No. 300 ("I abstain from all flourish & pomp of words").

Quite conclusive is the broad fact that the earlier notebook from the very start presupposes written work on immaterialism, and without it would be in large part unintelligible. Its opening pages build on the essay on time, and entries 1–16 look like an abstract of it; entries 17–26 presuppose extensive studies of the immaterial hypothesis, dealing with perceptual theory, primary and secondary qualities, the infinite divisibility of space and time, and the nature of the soul or person; from No. 27 onwards the *Essay on Vision*, more or less as we have it now, is in full view, and from the notebook as a whole (see below, p. 49) we know that the structure of the *Essay on Vision* was virtually complete, and the writing at an advanced stage. All these subjects bear directly on immaterialism; on all of them Berkeley speaks in the first two pages of the notebook. Moreover the things he says about them are not odd jottings or casual remarks by a tiro feeling his way; they are critical comments by a mature mind, moving with ease among familiar subjects; they are philosophical comments by a man who knows where he is going because he has been there before. In a word Berkeley could not have written on this network of subjects to do with immaterialism as he does in the opening pages of this notebook, unless he had already written extensively about them. This to justify my inclusion of the first arguings in the above list of Berkeley's early writings.

I will add some further introductory information about the early writings on time, vision and perceptual theory.

Entries on time occur in both notebooks, and *Time* is one of the indexed topics. Our knowledge of the essay rests on Berkeley's statement to his American friend, Samuel Johnson, coupled with the *en bloc* entries on time and eternity with which the *Commentaries* opens.

On 24 March 1730 Berkeley wrote to Johnson about his philosophy, and said, "One of my earliest inquiries was about Time, which led me into several paradoxes that I did not think fit or necessary to publish, particularly the notion that the Resurrection follows the next moment to death."* The rest of the letter makes it quite clear that the essay on time was an integral part of Berkeley's study of immaterialism. So do the early entries in the notebook. That time is the succession of ideas (No. 4), existing only in the mind (No. 13), and not outside as well (as Newton taught), is a vital part of the case against matter. The "paradoxes", unfit for publication, can be discerned in the *Commentaries*. The notion that the resurrection follows the next moment to death is the point of the story of Marsilius Ficinus (No. 390) and of Deering's question about the thief and paradise (No. 127).

Berkeley was not well satisfied, I fancy, with his essay on time, and he is careful to tell Johnson that in these matters every man is to think for himself. Probably the essay had a limited

* *Works*, Vol. II, p. 293.

scope, but served its turn, like the two sections (97, 98) on time in the *Principles*. By his study Berkeley assured himself that time does not postulate matter, and is not absolute, nor infinitely divisible. That was as far as he needed to go in his first arguings. The essay on time cleared the way for immaterialism, but left several points in doubt.

Turn now to the early writings on vision. These were part and parcel of his study of immaterialism. The *Essay on Vision* was published a year before the *Principles*; but the *Principles* was conceived first. Berkeley wished to argue that there are no bodies in external space; and he was met by the obvious rejoinder, "Yes, there are. I can see them." Till he had cleared up that difficulty by an analysis of seeing and the object seen, he could not make much headway with his main argument. He himself says in the *Principles* (section 43) that the difficulty about seeing external space and seeing bodies actually existing in it "gave birth to my *Essay towards a new Theory of Vision*".

Berkeley's work on vision must have reached an advanced stage during his Fellowship-candidate period, and it formed part of his first arguings. The contents of the earlier notebook presuppose a draft of the *Essay on Vision*, structurally identical with the published work except for the sections (122 ff.) on abstract ideas, which were added later, and the sections (88–120) on the inverted retinal image, which involved a modification of the original plan of the book. Entries on vision (Nos. 27, 28, 32) begin immediately after those on time and the immaterial hypothesis; there are some 150 of them in the one notebook, and in point of numbers of notes vision is the leading topic of the notebook. A few entries are observations on vision in general or on other people's opinions about it, but most of them are Berkeley's notes and queries on what he himself had already written on vision. Proofs are, (a) the marginal index which is full and specific, and (b) the contents of some entries which build on an existing draft work on vision, and apart from it would be meaningless.

Take the latter point first. Here is an entry which by itself is

D

gibberish, and becomes luminous in every word, read as a comment on the draft.

✗ 3a   *Query whether the sensations of sight arising from a man's head be liker the sensations of touch proceeding from thence or from his legs?*

(No. 224)

No man in his senses could have written that remark out of the blue. "Sensations of sight from the head" is a strange phrase; "sensations of sight from the legs" is grotesque; and why the juxtaposition with sensations of touch? The meaning and relevance jump to the eye when the entry is read as Berkeley's comment on his draft of the sections, now numbered 101 ff., in his *Essay on Vision*. He is on the problem of the inverted retinal image, and by way of illustration he imagines himself observing a man who is standing on the ground. He contrasts the observer's visual data of the observed man's head and legs with his corresponding tactual data, and argues that if we interpret the visual data as *signs* of the tactual data, the alleged inversion disappears.

I deal below (p. 56) with the system of marginal signs. Here I will only point out that this remarkable feature of the *Commentaries* as a whole is invaluable in the case of the entries on vision, and particularly instructive. Like the two-headed eagle it looks two ways, back to the draft and on to the publication. Throughout the *Commentaries* entries on vision have the marginal sign ✗ *plus a number*. The numbers used are 1, 2, 3 and 3a, and each number refers to a specific division of the work, as follows:

✗1   refers to the division on Distance (sections 2–51); e.g. Nos. 170, 501.

✗2   refers to the division on Magnitude (sections 52–87); e.g. Nos. 11, 125, 140 and others.

✗3   refers to the division on the heterogeneity of sight and touch (sections 121–46); e.g. No. 27 and many others.

✗³ᵃ refers to the division on Situation, i.e. on the inverted retinal image (sections 88–120); e.g. Nos. 102, 126 and eight others. The "a" indicates that this division was an afterthought. All the entries dealing with the inverted retinal image, and they only, have the "³ᵃ" sign. Berkeley inserted this division before the original third division, because he regarded the heterogeneity of sight and touch as the key to the solution of the problem of the inversion of the retinal image.

N.B. The numbers are placed irregularly in the manuscript; and often a stroke is added which is probably an indication of a "tick-off". It was not found possible to distinguish in the reproduction between this stroke and the number 1.

I must also deal with a pair of entries in which Berkeley refers to his draft work on vision, and indicates a fundamental weakness in its main argument, viz:

✗³ *Wt I have said onely proves there is no proportion at all times & in all men between a visible & tangible inch v.g.*

(No. 69)

✗³ *Tangible & visible extension heterogeneous because they have no common measure: also because their simplest, constituent parts or elements are specifically distinct viz. punctum visibile & tangibile. N.B. The former seems to be no good reason.*

(No. 70)

Both entries are on the heterogeneity of sight and touch; the point of the former entry is that Berkeley needed to prove an absolute heterogeneity; but on reading over his draft work he has to admit that he has only proved a relative heterogeneity. The difference between sight and touch had been impressed on Berkeley and his contemporaries by the "Molyneux problem" about the man born blind and made to see. Heterogeneity is mentioned in the first section of the *Essay on Vision*; it becomes increasingly prominent in the divisions on Distance and Magnitude; and from section 88 onward it dominates the *Essay*. In section 91 Berkeley accepts the heterogeneity of the two senses as the solution of the problem of the inverted retinal image, rejecting Descartes's solution. In section 111 he declares that "all visible things are equally in the mind, and take up no part of the external space: And consequently are equidistant from any tangible thing which exists without the mind". In sections 127–31 he handles the principle laid down in our entry (No. 69); he offers three proofs of the proposition that the ideas of sight are specifically distinct from the ideas of touch that are called by the same names. The third of these proofs is the impossibility of adding a visible line or surface to a tangible line or surface, and of comparing them "in the several ways of proportion". No one of the three proofs offered is very strong, and the third is distinctly weak and relative to particular cases, as Berkeley points out.

When he came to revise his earlier work on vision, Berkeley found that the heterogeneity of sight and touch, the foundation of his main argument, had been shown to be probable, but had not been proved true in all cases. It is a curious parallel to the radical weakness in the argument against matter, laid bare by the revision (see No. 265, discussed above, p. 46). In the case of his *Essay on Vision*, as in the case of the *Principles*, Berkeley's first arguings had taken him a certain distance, and had then failed him. In the latter case Berkeley was able to mend his hand; he found his "new principle" for disproving the existence of matter; in the former case he found no remedy, and had to be content with something less than proof.

The fact is that sight and touch are homogeneous *and* heterogeneous, and their heterogeneity cannot do the work that in his *Essay on Vision* Berkeley sought to make it do. In the *Principles* (section 44) their heterogeneity is asserted indeed, but is assigned a minor place, and virtually drops out of sight in the completed argument. Sight is not touch; visual data are not tactual data; we cannot see hardness or touch redness; sight and touch belong to different *genera*; they are heterogeneous. But on the other hand sight and touch are homogeneous; they both are senses; they both belong to the *genus sense*; visual *sensa* and *sensibilia* and tactual *sensa* and *sensibilia* are all on the same footing; they all are alike in that they are objects of sense and for sense. Berkeley's distinction is valid within the *ad interim* metaphysic of his *Essay on Vision*, but not outside. As long as he placed visible objects in the mind, and allowed his readers to think that tangible objects were outside the mind, as he does in section 111, he could maintain the heterogeneity of sight and touch; but as soon as he became consistent and released his full-blooded immaterialism, the half-hearted metaphysic of the *Essay on Vision* was left behind; all sensible objects alike were taken into the mind, and the heterogeneity of sight and touch *eo ipso* lost most of its former significance. The contribution of the *Essay on Vision* to general psychology and the psychology of vision can hardly be overstated; but its metaphysic was only a temporary expedient, and in discussing the making of the *Principles* that fact must be borne in mind.

Berkeley's earlier writings covered time, vision and the immaterial hypothesis with special reference to the sensible qualities of body. It is the same story in all three cases—a certain amount of progress and then a stone wall blocking advance. He wrote on time, went a certain distance, came up against dangerous paradoxes, and could get no further. He wrote on vision, and put together a fine book about it; but rigid proof of its basic assumption eluded his grasp. He wrote on the sensible qualities, on body and space, with a view to proving the non-existence of matter, and he was forced to admit that from Malebranche, Locke and his own first arguings it could not be *proved* (No. 265). Berkeley must have penned that entry with a pen of lead and a heavy heart, unless indeed he was already in sight of a better way, and unless his failures were proving the gateway to success.

Finally I come to the quarry where the present work was shaped, Berkeley's *Philosophical Commentaries*. These two notebooks stand high in philosophical literature for their wide range, the depth of their thought, and their systematic character. On first acquaintance they look simple, superficial and casual, and some general information about them is essential, if readers are to follow the detailed use made of them in the chapters that follow.

The notebooks, now in the British Museum (Add. MS. 39305), were found by Professor A. C. Fraser among the "Berkeley Papers" and were published by him nearly one hundred years ago. He found them bound in the wrong order, and he published them in the wrong order, and he gave them the misleading title, *The Commonplace Book of occasional metaphysical thoughts*. He and the philosophers of his day misunderstood the structure, scope and purpose of the work. It is not a commonplace book, nor are the metaphysical thoughts in it occasional. The contents of the notebooks are not casual or impromptu jottings; but they are for the most part Berkeley's systematic and critical comments on his own earlier work on immaterialism. Professor T. Lorenz found the key to the correct order of the notebooks. Dr. G. A. Johnston published an edition in 1930, greatly superior to Fraser's, but it, too, contained serious mistakes in the text and in the order of entries. In my *editio diplomatica* of 1944 I corrected the text and the order of entries, and made the change to the present title, which is now generally accepted.

The *Commentaries* is one two-fold work; sometimes its unity needs the stress, sometimes its duality. Practically all its 888 entries hinge on the immaterial hypothesis; and many of them look backward to the first arguings and forward to the *Principles*. Yet the two notebooks are *two*, and the second is not just a continuation of the first. The two notebooks cover similar ground; but the one carried out the first stages of the revision, and led up to a doctrinal discovery that revolutionized the thesis; while the other made a fresh start from that discovery, and built up the doctrinal detail of the revised system.

When the two notebooks have to be compared or contrasted

or spoken of separately, how shall we designate them? We cannot continue to speak of "the one" and "the other". "First" and "second" will not do; for they have been bound and continuously foliated in the wrong order, with the result that what was first to the writer, the binder has made second, and *vice versa*. The labels *first* and *second* are therefore ambiguous and misleading. There is nothing for it but to continue the designations used in the *editio diplomatica* (p. xvii), and speak of "notebook B" and "notebook A". It is a tiresome usage at first, but I see no help for it.* I have to ask the reader to remember that if AB is the composite volume on the shelves of the British Museum, then B is the notebook filled first by Berkeley, and placed second by the binder, and foliated accordingly, and A is the notebook filled second by Berkeley and placed first by the binder, and foliated accordingly. To put it graphically:

Notebook B was written first, and contains folios 104–164,

and

Notebook A was written second, and contains folios 3–95.

The main work of the revision was done on the *recto*, and most of the *verso* pages are blank. With two exceptions (160 v and 164 v) they were all left blank originally. When substantial corrections or important comments had to be made, Berkeley made them as a rule on the facing page. The letter *a* after the number of the entry in my numeration indicates a correction or comment *on the verso* opposite the entry *on the recto*. In many cases the *verso* entries were made weeks or months after the corresponding *recto* entries, and represent later stages in the revision.

If my reasoning is correct, as I believe it to be, notebook B was begun in July or August 1707, and was more or less completed by November or December of that year; and notebook A

* Unless indeed the British Museum would take Professor Furlong's suggestion, and rebind them in the right order.

was begun shortly before the completion of notebook B, and was finished in August 1708.*

The marginal apparatus of letters and signs which runs from the first page to the last is a striking feature of the *Commentaries*. One glance at it shows that this is no haphazard collection of philosophical jottings; but a serious work with a purpose. The apparatus was Berkeley's system of reference; it must have been invaluable to him in his revising, and it is still very useful to the reader who understands it.

Two signs are used, ✕ and ✚. The ✕ *with a number* denotes entries on vision, as explained above (p. 50). The ✕ *plain* denotes mathematics in a broad sense, as is clear from the margins of Nos. 676 and 853. The *plus* sign ✚ stands before entries which Berkeley found he could not use, in a few cases because they are trivial or personal, in many cases because they contain views he no longer held. In effect the sign was an obelus, and it is of great importance in our study of development and revision; for it calls attention to Berkeley's discarded views.

Berkeley himself indexed the *letters* he used, and assigned their meanings, on folio 3 at the beginning of notebook A. The letter E in the index epitomizes the main course of the revision; completely absent from notebook B and introduced in notebook A, it indicates Berkeley's discovery towards the end of notebook B of the nature and meaning of *Existence*, and of the new turn, thereby given, to his philosophy.

I now give a table, based on Berkeley's index of the letters, to show the distribution of topics between the notebooks. The chief points of interest are, (1) the even distribution of entries on *Matter* and the *Qualities*, (2) the overwhelming preponderance in notebook A of entries on *Soul* and *Spirit*, and (3) the absence from notebook B of entries marked E for *Existence*. The large

---

* For the dating and other particulars about the notebooks see my Introduction to the *editio diplomatica*, London, 1944. My general conclusions about the date have been remarkably confirmed by the recent discovery of the dated copy of the "Of Infinites". See above, p. 44, and *Works*, Vol. IX, p. 158.

number of entries marked S *erased* in notebook B should be noted. The S there probably stood for *Space*; it may represent a specialist study of space and sensible qualities that was superseded by the discovery of the Principle, thus releasing the letter S for *Soul* and *Spirit*. I have not been able to satisfy myself on the point.

	DISTRIBUTION OF MARGINAL LETTERS AND SIGNS	NOTEBOOK B	A
I	Introduction	4	59
I	(erased) „	1	25
M	Matter	62	66
P	Primary & Secondary Qualities	17	18
E	Existence	0	29
T	Time	11	3
S	Soul—Spirit	11	120
S	(erased) ? Space	*c.* 39	0
G	God	5	15
Mo	Moral Philosophy	5	44
N	Natural Philosophy	8	26
✕ (plain)	Mathematics	106	102
✕ (with numbers)	*Essay on Vision*	91	11
+	Obelus	123	65

The notebooks were of great use to Berkeley; and they have been of some use to his readers. Writers have quoted from them to illustrate isolated points of doctrine; but few have attempted to read between the lines, and determine the course of the doctrinal development they represent and record. They are difficult documents, and a pre-requisite of success in studying them is to get beneath the surface, and treat the work as a systematic composition with a definite end in view throughout. When you meet a difficulty, said Malebranche, put the problem in query form; abridge your ideas and get them down on paper, and you will discover a principle to solve your problem. In the spirit of those Rules of Method Berkeley wrote the *Commentaries*; he dedicated a year's sustained thought to the task of revising his original thesis; his problem was to find a principle which would supply what his first arguings lacked, viz. a valid basis for denying the existence of matter, and of building on that basis a consistent philosophy. To use his own simile (No. 521) Berkeley throughout these notebooks is the seeker after truth hunting the one long trail.

The trail is there, but it is hard to find. One gets the impression of a doctrinal jungle on first turning the pages of the notebooks. To correct that impression two externals should be noted—the comparative uniformity of the whole series of 888 entries, and the marginal apparatus of signs and letters, described above. Each entry has a well-marked beginning and ending, and almost every one of them has its place in the argument, evidenced by its marginal sign or letter. Plan and purpose are in evidence throughout from the first page (f. 104) with its impressive observations on time and eternity, duly indexed, to the final pages (ff. 94, 95) where similar entries, similarly indexed, are rounded off with the date, August 28th 1708, and with a sententious quotation, expressive of young ambition. There are many side issues in the notes, of temporary importance to Berkeley, but not to our purpose. Of pendulum clocks, mirrors and glasses, of surds, concentric circles and fluxions, of Newton's theories of colour, space, time and motion, of the arguments for and against the infinite divisibility, of psychological and ethical questions, and of natural phenomena, studied by Berkeley for his projected Books II and III, we shall take no account in the present work. The wide variety of topics is evidence of Berkeley's thoroughness; they are all connected directly or indirectly with immaterialism; but many of them are side issues, only distantly related to Berkeley's central line of development. Our business is with that central line. We shall watch what Berkeley kept and what he threw away. We shall watch the slow and steady development of his thought about matter and the sensible, about the meaning and nature of existence, about abstract ideas, about body, mind and God.

CHAPTER IV

LOCKE, MALEBRANCHE AND BAYLE

AMONG the many authorities mentioned in the *Commentaries* Locke, Malebranche and Bayle are of outstanding importance. When Berkeley was filling the notebooks, copies of Locke's *Essay* and of Taylor's translation of Malebranche's *Recherche* must have been on his study table, with a volume or two of Bayle's Dictionary.

Locke's *Essay* was Berkeley's grammar; from it he learned the groundwork of philosophy; in it he met the leading concepts and the standing problems; there he read of mind and body, of space, time and motion, of matter, of substance, of cause and effect, of idea and ideate, of primary and secondary qualities, of freedom and necessity, of perception and thinking, of being and knowing. There is hardly a page in the *Commentaries* but testifies to Locke's influence; yet Locke had little to say to the distinctive elements in Berkeley's philosophy. Locke's *Essay* taught Berkeley, but did not make Berkeley what he was.

Malebranche's *Recherche* was the irritant, the grit that made the pearl. Malebranche gave point and direction to Berkeley's search for truth, gave him his theme and lofty outlook, led him to an untenable immaterialism, and left him there high and dry.

"Locke taught him, but Malebranche inspired him." I see no reason to alter that judgment I passed nearly thirty years ago,* but perhaps it needs a balance; and today I would add, "Bayle alarmed and alerted him." The evidence that Malebranche deeply influenced Berkeley in his young days is incontrovertible. Malebranche put immaterialism into his head; there was no one else to do it; yet every single mention of Malebranche in the

---

* *Berkeley and Malebranche* (Oxford, 1934), p. 7. Even then I was aware that Bayle was an important influence, ranking next to Malebranche and Locke, see ib., pp. 53 ff.

Commentaries is in adverse criticism or in downright opposition. The explanation is simple. Malebranche inspired his first arguings. Bayle provoked his second thoughts. Berkeley originally conceived the immaterial hypothesis within the framework of Malebranche's philosophy; his first immaterialism was Malebranchian. Bayle's articles on *Pyrrho* and *Zeno* opened his eyes to the sceptical trends of Malebranche's philosophy apart from Malebranche's religion. Berkeley took alarm, turned against the source of his first inspiration, became severely critical of it, began to examine and revise his previous writings, and in the course of the revision found the doctrine of the *Principles*.

Locke's *Essay* was well established in Trinity College at the turn of the century when Berkeley entered. It was on the course within two years of its publication through the influence of William Molyneux, Locke's friend and correspondent. Peter Browne, the Provost, a philosopher of distinction, accepted critically "the new way of ideas". In his notebooks Berkeley refers to the *Essay* over and over again, and speaks of Locke in the highest terms; but he does not speak as a Lockeian. There was no party line, or official philosophy, for him. He was free to think for himself, and could question almost anything. He came with an open mind to the problems of knowledge, perception and the external world.

Berkeley did not learn to doubt or deny the existence of matter from Locke. There are seeds of general doubt in the *Essay*, and the fourth Book leaves the external world in an ambiguous position; but Locke nowhere challenges the existence of matter. He frankly accepted matter, and admitted "the possibility of matter's thinking".* With the press and the pulpit and most of his contemporaries Locke conceded that secondary qualities are in the mind, in the sense that there is nothing like them in the object; all the more firmly he held on to matter and the external thing, composed of primary qualities.

Locke's theory of sense-perception underlies much of Berkeley's argument in notebook B. Locke teaches that the immediate

* *Essay* IV, iii, 6; the passage was noted by Berkeley in PC No. 695.

object of perception is an idea, and that the power to produce an idea in our minds is a quality of the subject wherein that power is. I see a snowball, and I see it white and round; the subject "snowball" has the power to produce those ideas or qualities in us; the snowball may be regarded either as a collection of active powers or as a collection of passive beings.*

Locke recognizes two classes of qualities or powers, primary and secondary; with some hesitation he adds a third class, tertiary. The primary qualities or powers are original and utterly inseparable from the body; they are powers in the body to produce in us the ideas of solidity, extension, figure, motion or rest, and number. The secondary qualities are not real; they are nothing in the objects themselves; they are powers to produce sensations in us; and this they do by means of their primary qualities, i.e. by the bulk, figure, texture and motion of their insensible parts. The tertiary qualities (if they exist) are powers in inanimate things to make changes in other inanimate things, such as the supposed power in fire to melt wax.

Locke's external world is peopled with "powers", and Berkeley's treatment of these mysterious pockets of activity forms an important part of his doctrinal development.†

Locke's use of the terms *idea, quality* and *power* is vague and inconsistent. Sometimes he identifies them; at other times he keeps them separate. He discusses whether the idea is like, or unlike, its ideate; and he teaches that the ideas of primary qualities are like those qualities, while the ideas of secondary qualities are unlike them.

Berkeley was well grounded in Locke's ideism; but he departed from it on several important points while filling his notebooks; for instance, he gave up Locke's abstract general ideas, Locke's ultimate "simple ideas", and ideas of powers or active beings. Moreover two cardinal points of Locke's system, viz. no significant words without ideas, and no knowledge without ideas, formally accepted by Berkeley towards the end of note-

* *Essay* II, viii; cf. PC No. 113.
† See below, p. 133.

book B (No. 378) are rejected later. In section 24 of the Introduction to the *Principles* (cf. *Alciphron*, VII, 8 ff.) Berkeley accepts
emotive words without ideational content; and in No. 730
knowledge without ideas, viz. of spirits, is explicitly asserted.

Berkeley learned much from Locke in minor matters; for the
source of his immaterialism we must look elsewhere. He was a
bold and original thinker; but we cannot suppose that it would
have occurred to him when he was in his teens to challenge the
tradition of two thousand years, unless some authority had put
the idea into his head. The evidence that Malebranche did so is
full and strong. The evidence must be considered in its context
and entirety; for Berkeley in his plastic days learned from
Malebranche a good deal else besides immaterialism.*

The *Essay on Vision* owes much to the first book of the
Recherche, especially to Chapter vi, which is mentioned in the
Commentaries (Nos. 255 and 257) and subsequent chapters. Many
principles used in the *Essay* for which Berkeley commonly gets

---

* I assembled the evidence in my *Berkeley and Malebranche*. To the evidence
there presented should now be added the notice of Berkeley's books in the
"Mémoires de Trévoux" for May and December 1713, recently unearthed
by H. M. Bracken, and published in his *The Early Reception of Berkeley's
Immaterialism*, 1710–13 (The Hague, 1959). The reviewer describes
Berkeley as "Malebranchiste de bonne foi". The term "Malebranchiste" is
not exact, and the review is hostile to both thinkers; but it is contemporary
evidence for the connection between them. The difference between the two
thinkers is just as important as the connection, as I have never ceased
to urge.

The objection that Berkeley nowhere admits in terms his debt to Malebranche is answered by practical considerations. Berkeley had to think of
his bread and butter, and Malebranche was a French monk, suspected of
"enthusiasm", who had published hostile statements about Britain and the
British Crown.

The objection from the passage in the second Dialogue (*Works*, Vol. II,
p. 214) is completely answered by a careful study of the facts. The fundamental opposition of which Berkeley there speaks is a fact; so too is the
partial agreement there implied. The passage should be read first in the first
edition; the long addition in the 1734 edition was probably due to the fact
that during the twenty years' interval Berkeley had become a public figure,
and he may have had public reasons for dissociating his teaching from
that of the Oratorian.

the credit, came to him *via* the *Recherche*. Such are, the dual character of judgments of perception, the "mediums" in judgments of distance, the comparison of sense-data to language, the non-necessary character of the connection of ideas, and the contrast between conventional connections and the universal connections established by the will of God.

Berkeley mentions Malebranche for the first time, as stated above (p. 42), in his *De ludo algebraico*, published in 1707 in his *Miscellanea Mathematica*, but probably written much earlier. He appeals to Malebranche for support, and praises algebra almost in the words of Malebranche. Berkeley and Malebranche both call algebra a universal science, the key science, and the foundation of the sciences, and both speak of the limitless range of knowledge opened up by the algebraic method. More important is the unstinted praise that Berkeley proceeds to give to Malebranche's rules of method; "angelic rules" they had been called, and Berkeley quotes the phrase with evident relish. Malebranche sets out these rules in the first chapter of Part II of his sixth book, and he promises the discovery of "an infallible principle" to those who practise them. The chief rules are, (1) put the problem in query form, (2) be on the watch for intermediate ideas, (3) isolate the problem, and analyse it, (4) abridge your ideas and get them down on paper. Berkeley practised these rules. All four are exemplified in the *Commentaries*. The query-form is prominent in both notebooks. Eighty-six entries are introduced by "Qu."; some forty more ask questions. Intermediate ideas are discussed in Nos. 447, 697, 698 and 729. Themes such as cause, power, identity, understanding and will are carefully analysed. The abridgment of ideas is strikingly exemplified in many pages of the notebooks; the point, pith and brevity of the earlier entries are marked features, and halfway through notebook B Berkeley's New Principle was discovered, as if in fulfilment of Malebranche's promise. The notebooks exemplify and embody his rules of method.

The following entries, Nos. 265, 288, 288a, 358, 424, 686,

686a, 800 and 818, show Berkeley's attention to Malebranche's argument about matter. Some of them, viz. Nos. 265, 288, 288a and 358 (with 424) imply that Berkeley had been persuaded at first by that argument, and then was not satisfied with it, and sought and found a better argument. The *locus classicus* of immaterialism, viz. Malebranche's excursus on matter, is named or referred to in Nos. 686, 686a, 800 and 818.

I will now discuss this excursus at some length; for at one bound it places readers today in that universe of thought that yielded Berkeley's immaterialism and the revision we are to study.

Malebranche was not an immaterialist; but this excursus of his paves the way to immaterialism for those who are not of his religious persuasion. He based belief in matter and material body and a world external to the mind on the faith of his Church, not on reason. He took a seed of doubt from Descartes's fertile garden, reared it in a hothouse of his own, grew from it an all-spiritual world, without matter or sensible body, and said to his readers in effect, Behold the fruits of reason without faith.

The excursus or *éclaircissement* is appended with many others to the *Recherche*; in Taylor's translation it bears the title, "That 'tis very difficult to prove the Existence of Bodies; what we ought to esteem of the proofs which are brought of their existence." This excursus was known to Berkeley and his English contemporaries as the "Illustration". Taylor regularly uses that term to translate *éclaircissement*; and so does the translator of Bayle's article *Zeno*, which mentions this particular excursus. J. Keill refers to it by that name, saying "the oftner I read his long Illustration . . ."* Berkeley refers to it by that name in the *Commentaries*:

M.P.E.   *Malbranch in his Illustration differs widely from me He doubts of the existence of Bodies I doubt not in the least of this.*

(No. 800)

* J. Keill, *Examination of Dr. Burnet's Theory of the Earth* (Oxford, 1698), p. 8.

Earlier Berkeley had sketched the results of the excursus, saying

+   *Scripture & possibility are the onely proofs with*
      Malbranch add to these wt he calls a great propension
      to think so . . .

                                   (from No. 686, cf. 818)

With which must be read the comment on the facing page,
which throws a flood of light on the mode and motive of the
revision.

M   *On second thoughts I am, on t'other extream I am certain*
      of that wch Malbranch seems to doubt of. viz the exist-
      ence of Bodies.

                                   (No. 686a)

Malebranche wrote this excursus to elucidate his statement,
"We often see things that have no existence, nor ever had, and
it ought not to be concluded that a thing is actually without us
from our seeing it without us."* On the face of it it is an absurd
statement; for if we see things they exist, and if they do not
exist they cannot be seen. Malebranche would justify the paradox by the distinction between *voir* and *regarder*, and the distinction between the immediate object and the mediate. With
the eye of the flesh, he would say, we see (*voir*) the colour of the
wax; with the eye of the mind we see (*regarder*) the material
body *wax*. Now in illusions, hallucinations and dreams *ex hypothesi* there is no material body, and yet the senses function as if
there were. In such cases, Malebranche held, we are seeing
things that have no existence.

Now the rationalist in the Oratorian could not leave the
matter there; if in truth we are entitled to say that we see things
that have no existence, it certainly becomes very hard to prove
the existence of bodies. If in dreams I can see things that are not
there, why not also in sense-perception? How can I be sure of
any Body? If I can have a visual experience without material
backing *once*, why not *twice* and *often*—and indeed *always*? If I

† *Recherche*, Book I, 10, cf. Book VI, ii, 6.

can see the colour of the material body, though there is no
material body, is there any justification for believing in the
existence of the material body? Is there a material body? Does
matter exist?

True to his starting-point Malebranche divides human knowledge into two types, sense-perception which stems from the
soul's union with the body, and rational knowledge which
arises from the soul's union with the Word of God. Does either
source, he asks, guarantee the existence of material body?

With regard to sense-perception his answer is clear and unambiguous. There is no conclusive reason for trusting the
senses. The testimony of the senses, he says, is never exactly
true, and often quite false. The senses tell us that colours are on
bodies, sounds in the air, heat in the fire, and odour in the
musk; and yet all those qualities are in the soul that feels them.
Men feel pain in limbs that have been amputated, and the
moon seen with the naked eye is one thing, seen through a glass
is another thing. For these and similar reasons, Malebranche
argues, the evidence of sense for the existence of matter must be
inconclusive. When we see sensible bodies we see *them*; we are
not entitled to proceed further; we are not entitled to judge that
there are material bodies outside the mind, and that they are
like the sensible bodies we see.

Malebranche then turns to the evidence of reason, and asks
whether God has given us a rational assurance of the existence
of matter. His answer is hesitant and not quite consistent. It
amounts to, "By faith, Yes. By reason, on the whole, No." He
is clear that material bodies exist for faith, and that their existence is part of the setting of the Christian faith. He says, "We
cannot deny the existence of bodies through a principle of religion." Whatever exactly he means by the words, they leave the
impression that but for Christian dogma he would have denied
outright the existence of material body. He states explicitly that
we are not "invincibly carried to believe there is anything existing besides God and our own mind". He admits with Descartes
that God has given us a strong inclination to believe in matter;

but he qualifies the admission in several ways. This inclination works through sensible impressions, which are fallible. Moreover an inclination is not a compulsion. If we believe that matter exists, *we* believe it, not God in us; the most we can say is that there is more reason to hold that matter exists than to hold that it does not exist.

The excursus is a frank utterance by an honest thinker, drawn one way by his creed and another way by his reason. It has a certain balance for balanced readers; but that the general trend of it is towards a panpsychist immaterialism cannot be denied. Its phrasing is forcible, and it could not fail to impress a fearless young thinker, like Berkeley, who shared the author's philosophical approach, but had a different religious outlook.

"I was obliged to prove that there are stronger objections [to the argument for the existence of matter] than those of Malebranche." With this quotation we pass on from Malebranche to Bayle. Berkeley must have paused and thought of many things, when he first read those words. He read them in the article *Zeno* in Bayle's Dictionary. I have long known that Bayle influenced Berkeley; but the nature of that influence, and its significance in the making of Berkeley's immaterialism, came home to me when I read the writing of Professor R. H. Popkin on continental scepticism.* Popkin has argued forcibly that historians of British philosophy have neglected the scepticism of the continent, and have overlooked its many-sided character. Berkeley's broadsides against scepticism are usually taken as routine attacks on atheists and unbelievers; they have in fact deeper roots and are organically connected with the evolution of his own philosophy; they spring from his personal contact with continental scepticism, by which he was attracted and repelled, and influenced, first positively and then negatively. Continental scepticism was an attitude, not a creed; it had various objectives, and took various forms; on the whole it

* Especially "The Sceptical Crisis and the rise of modern philosophy" in the *The Review of Metaphysics* (September 1953), and "Berkeley and Pyrrhonism", ib., V, pp. 223–46.

was more concerned for freedom than concerned with truth; it was more concerned with doubting knowledge than with doubting or denying the existence of God; it was not necessarily irreligious; indeed Montaigne and Malebranche and Bayle himself use scepticism at times in defence of institutional religion.

Pierre Bayle (1647–1706) is an enigma. Born a Protestant, son of a Calvinist divine, he joined the Church of Rome for a year or two, and then reverted to Protestantism. He knew the arguments on both sides; he saw two sides in almost every question. His Dictionary has two sides; it combines indecent and salacious passages with pure intellectual work of the highest order. The general aim of the annotations is to inculcate scepticism; but often one cannot tell whether Bayle is giving his own views, or arguing upon the principles of others, or, indeed, arguing irresponsibly *pro et con* for the fun of arguing. His Dictionary, first published in 1695–7, came out in an enlarged edition in 1702. It was the most comprehensive expression of continental scepticism, and soon became extremely influential. A copy of it was sold at the auction of the Berkeleys' library.*

Bayle is named in the *Commentaries* in a duplicated entry (Nos. 358, 424) which brackets him with Malebranche, and declares that their arguments prove against bodies but not against space. Bayle is named in *The Theory of Vision Vindicated* (1733), section 6, and is there described as an atheist. What Berkeley's feelings were towards Bayle at the earlier period is not on record; probably they were mixed. Bayle dots the 'i's and crosses the 't's of Malebranche, and in his hands immaterialism takes on a new look. The "stronger arguments" against matter that Bayle mentions are, (1) that all the arguments brought against the reality of the secondary qualities apply with equal force to the primary qualities, and (2) that the mathematical arguments for infinite divisibility are either false or prove that extension does not exist without the mind. Both these arguments appear in the *Commentaries* (Nos. 20, 26,

* R. I. Aaron, *Mind*, XLI (N.S.), p. 461.

236). From Bayle, Berkeley learned the full force of his first argument against matter, and from the same source and about the same time he learned that French immaterialism skirts the edge of a precipice. To doubt the existence of the world is the most radical doubt of all; atheism is curable; confirmed acosmism not.

In the following entry from the early part of the *Commentaries* Berkeley expresses his fear. The correction is significant:

M   *Mem. that I take notice that I do not fall in wth Sceptics Fardella etc, in yt I make bodies to exist certainly* (prima manu *wthout us*) *wch they doubt of.*

(No. 79)

In his article *Zeno* Bayle records that Fardella in 1695 printed at Venice a Logic in which he asserted the same doctrine as Malebranche, viz. that objects may not be like their ideas, and that God may have so disposed our senses that they represent as existing non-existent things; and that if we believe in the existence of bodies, it is by faith alone. Arnauld attacked this thesis, says Bayle, and he adds that the inquisitors of Italy did not proceed against Fardella, nor the Sorbonne against Malebranche.

Michel-Angelo Fardella of Sicily was a Franciscan monk, a physicist and philosopher. In addition to the Logic which Bayle mentions, he wrote *Universae philosophiae systema* (1691), *Universae usualis mathematicae theoria* (1691), and *Animae humanae natura* (1698). His case and Berkeley's had much in common. Both were religious men, lovers of knowledge and seekers after truth; and both were brought by Malebranche's teaching to the brink of scepticism. Berkeley was alive to the danger, and realized that the existence of bodies is the crux. The erasure shows that he had a mind to assert against the sceptics the indubitable existence of bodies, but could not yet see his way to assert their externality; so he crossed out "without us" and substituted "certainly".

I will now trace the influence of specific articles in the Dictionary, beginning with the *Anaxagoras*. Anaxagoras was a Greek thinker who postulated the existence of germ-like elements, called *homoiomeries*; it looks like an attempt at a biological explanation of change; a thing is made up, he said, of little things like it; a tree is made up of little trees; a drop of blood is made up of little drops of blood, and so on. Bayle says that Anaxagoras postulated homoiomeries in order to avoid having to postulate a creation. Berkeley, too, finds them "useful to contemplate" (No. 64) and connects them with the creation (No. 60). Curiously Berkeley at first wrote "homoeomeries" in both those entries, and subsequently substituted "Homogeneous particles" in No. 60, and "Homogeneous portions of matter" in No. 64. Bayle styles them "homogeneities".

Bayle's article *Pyrrho* must be considered at length. It had a strong influence on Berkeley's thought, and from it many points found their way into Berkeley's books and notebooks. Its main theme is the scepticism of "modern philosophers", especially the Cartesians including Malebranche. The ancient sceptics declared that the sensible qualities of bodies are mere appearances, and that, for example, we feel heat in the presence of the fire, but do not know what the fire is, or whether *it* is hot. The moderns go further along the same road, saying that the sensible qualities are modifications of the soul, and that, for example, *we* are hot and not the fire. With his eye on Bayle's argument and instance, Berkeley declares in the *Commentaries* that the wall is white and the fire hot (No. 19), and sarcastically observes (No. 392) that we Irish men cannot attain to these truths, viz. "the wall is not white, the fire is not hot, &c".*

The *Pyrrho* proceeds to discuss the assimilation of the primary and secondary qualities.† This step was of great importance to

* See also the opening of the Introduction of the *Principles* and sections 14, 88, with 99 (1st. ed.) "those odd paradoxes, that the fire is not hot, nor the wall white, etc."

† For a masterly historical note on the distinction see *The Works of Thomas Reid, D.D.*, ed. Sir W. Hamilton, 6th ed. (Edinburgh, 1863), Vol. II, p. 825, Note D, where the following points are noted: The distinction is as

Berkeley, and he often gets the credit for it; but he was not the inventor; he found it in Bayle who took it from Simon Foucher. Bayle says that the moderns "would willingly have excepted extension and motion, but could not do it; for if the objects of the senses appear to us coloured, hot, cold, and emit an odour, though they really are not so, why might they not appear to have extension and figure, at rest and in motion, though there should really be no such thing". In a further note Bayle says that Foucher proposed this objection in his critique of the *Recherche*, and that Malebranche made no reply to it, knowing that it was unanswerable.

Simon Foucher, Canon of Dijon, an experimental scientist, author of *Traité des Hygromètres* (1686), published at Paris in 1675 his *Critique de la Recherche de la vérité*. In it he argues with force that Malebranche's arguments about the sensible or secondary qualities apply equally to the mathematical or primary qualities; that the objectivity of the primary qualities is no better founded than that of the secondary; that we know extension by direct perception just as we know colour; that extension, like colour, is a sensation, and sensations are modes of being of our souls. Descartes and Malebranche say that God would be a deceiver if there were no extended world outside; but He would be no less a deceiver, if there were no coloured world outside. Further the same object presents qualities of both types at the same time; the extended is also coloured; and if the colours are in us, so too are the shape and spread of the colours.

---

old as the Greeks. It is found in some shape or form in Leucippus, Democritus, Plato and Aristotle. Galileo, *Saggiatore* (1623) makes the distinction, and speaks of "primi e reali" qualities which reside in external objects, and tastes, odours, colours etc. which reside in the sentient subject; those of the former class are inseparable from the object. Locke took his crisp pair of opposing terms from Boyle, who in his *The origin of forms and qualities* (Oxford, 1666), speaks of "primitive modes or primary affections of bodies", distinguishing them from "less simple qualities that belong to bodies upon their account"; cf. his *Tracts*, 1671, pp. 18, 44, where "the Primary and most simple affections of matter" are distinguished from "the secondary qualities if I may so call them".

Foucher's aim in developing this powerful line of argument was to curb the dogmatism of the Cartesians by promoting the tempered scepticism of the Academics. Neither he nor Bayle was interested in immaterialism; neither he nor Bayle shared Berkeley's interest in the assimilation of the two types of qualities. They saw it as a rod in pickle for the Cartesians, and perhaps they saw what Berkeley was to learn, viz. that the assimilation does not *prove* the non-existence of matter.

On the finiteness of the mind of man and the inferences to be drawn from it Berkeley found much to his purpose in the *Pyrrho* article. Finiteness is a two-edged weapon, and Bayle uses it both to silence sceptics and support them. Our faculties are so weak and their range so limited that we can be sure of nothing, but must doubt everything. Again, our faculties are so weak and their range is so limited, that we cannot trust the reasonings of the sceptics; we must doubt doubt, must abandon the search for truth by reason, must pray to God for faith, shut our eyes and obey the Church. Bayle argues that Christianity itself contradicts the laws of evidence, instancing the doctrines of the Holy Trinity, of the Incarnation and of transubstantiation, and on that passage he has a note discriminating between transubstantiation and the other two doctrines. In the spirit of that note Berkeley writes:

+   *The Loss of the excuse may hurt Transubstantiation, but not the Trinity.*

                              (No. 350, cf. Nos. 584, 720)

On the facing page Berkeley explains "the excuse"; it is the finiteness of our minds. He met "the excuse" in physics and mathematics, as well as in theology and metaphysics, and he has devoted a good deal of attention to it both in his notebooks and in the *Principles*.*

Striking entries in the notebooks connect Berkeley's Principle,

---

* See PC 292, 323, 350, 350a, 747, 859–60, and *Principles*, Intro. 2, 3, and section 101 in the body of the work.

esse est percipi, and the new turn it gave to his philosophy, with his fear of scepticism and his discovery of the cure:

M   *The Reverse of ye Principle introduc'd Scepticism.*
                                                    (No. 304)

The reverse of the Principle is, of course, *esse est non-percipi*. The entry is repeated with amplification in No. 411, where scepticism, folly, contradictions and absurdities are traced to the same source.

Again, pointing out that many ancient philosophers ran into absurdities, even denying the existence of motion—an allusion to the *Zeno* article—Berkeley writes:

E   *. . . this sprung from their not knowing wt existence was*
           and wherein it consisted this the source of all their Folly,
           'tis on the Discovering of the nature & meaning &
           import of Existence that I chiefly insist. This puts a
           wide difference betwixt the Sceptics & me . . .
                                                    (from No. 491)

Scepticism about the external world, the fear of scepticism, and the recovery from scepticism clearly played a large part in young Berkeley's intellectual development, influencing both his first arguings and his second thoughts. Bayle's article *Pyrrho* must have been his main source of information about continental scepticism, and therefore an important factor in the making of his revised immaterialism.

Before we leave the *Pyrrho* article let me mention a passage in it that explains, I think, Berkeley's cryptic remark:

+   *Ignorance in some sort requisite in ye Person that should*
           Discover the Principle.
                                                    (No. 285)

Berkeley was proud of his discovery, and it is paradoxical that he should attribute it to ignorance. The German commentator, Professor Lorenz, felt the difficulty so keenly that he thought up the brilliant conjecture "disaver" for "discover". His brilliance was wasted, however; for Berkeley wrote "discover", and did not write "disaver".

The key is to be found, I suggest, in Bayle's cynical reference to ignorance in his clever section where he insinuates scepticism by showing how harmless and ineffective scepticism is, and quotes the saying, attributed to Simonides, "these men are not cunning enough to be imposed upon by such a person as I." Society has nothing to fear from scepticism, says Bayle. Most people have not the brains to be sceptics; they cannot keep sceptical arguments in their heads, and they do not understand the rules of wordy warfare. The sceptic always loses; he is like the general who lost the battle because (so he said) his enemy did not understand the art of war. Bayle continues, "The grace of God in the faithful, the forces of education in other men, perhaps ignorance and the natural inclination to be peremptory are a natural buckler against the darts of the sceptics."

When Berkeley attributed his discovery to "ignorance", he was not posing as an *ignoramus*. In a reminiscent mood he was meditating on the road he had travelled, and his narrow escapes. He said to himself, "I went far with Malebranche and Bayle. What kept me from going further? I made colour and heat mental, and extension, figure and motion; what kept me from permanently denying the existence of body and the external world? What held me back? It must have been that 'ignorance' of which Bayle speaks, that simplicity and unsophisticated approach which shield the mob from scepticism. I side in all things with the mob. The mob does not believe in matter and does believe in the world of sense. With them I hold that the things I see and touch are there to see and touch, and do not go in and out of existence with every turn of my perceivings. All I did was to ask the homely question, What *is* existence? What does the term *existence* mean? I gave the common-sense reply. That's how my discovery came about."

We pass on to Bayle's article *Zeno*, which was a major influence on a narrow front. *Zeno* contributed two specific arguments to Berkeley's armoury, (*a*) an analysis of the composition of extension, and (*b*) a refutation of infinite divisibility.

After a brief account of the antinomies of motion, attributed to Zeno, Bayle tries to present Zeno's problem in terms of contemporary thought. Those who wish to revive Zeno's opinion, he says, ought to argue thus:

There is no extension; therefore there is no motion.

He adds, with assumed naïveté, "The only difficulty is to prove that there is no extension"; and from this point on he concentrates on the nature and composition of extension, which he virtually identifies with matter, as Berkeley himself sometimes does. Infinite divisibility is the crux of the argument. Bayle rejects the infinite divisibility of time, treating the question cursorily, as Berkeley does,* and then devotes a long and subtle discussion to the nature of extension. Bayle begins by laying down a rule of method, designed to promote the sceptical attitude. We ought to proceed, he says, on the lines of a hypothetical syllogism, not a disjunctive. We ought not to argue that extension must consist of *a* or *b* or *c*; for that assumes that there is such a thing as extension. We ought rather to argue that if extension exists, it must consist of *a* or *b* or *c*. Berkeley took that rule seriously to heart. He uses the hypothetical form explicitly at least six times in the opening pages of notebook B (Nos. 40, 55, 65, 67, 68 and 81), and by implication many more times; he relates extension logically and hypothetically to one of Bayle's alternatives, when he argues:

✕   *Infinite divisibility of extension does suppose ye external existence of extension but the later is false, ergo ye former also.*

(No. 26)

The three alternatives for Bayle are mathematical points, or atoms, or parts divisible *in infinitum*. If there is such a thing as extension outside the mind, then, he argues, it must be

* See PC Nos. 8, 10, and *Principles*, section 98.

composed of one or other of those three. There is nothing very distinctive about the historical atom in that connection, and Berkeley has little or nothing to say about it; his *minimum sensibile* is in effect a sensible atom; but he deals at length with the other two alternatives, and follows Bayle's treatment closely. Bayle eliminates mathematical points on the ground that they are "nothings", and Berkeley makes great play with the same conception. Here is the opening of his attack on the "nothings":

✗   *The not Leading men into mistakes no argument for the truth of the infinitesimals. they being nothings may, perhaps, do neither good nor harm. except wn they are taken for somthing: & then the contradiction begets a Contradiction.*

(No. 337)

✗ $a + 500$ *nothings* $= a + 50$ *nothings an innocent silly truth.*

(No. 338)

Berkeley even coins the term "Nihilarian" for the mathematician, though on grounds of courtesy he decides not to use it (see Nos. 372, 399, 471, 633). In No. 394 he refers to the mathematicians' description of their point as "not altogether nothing nor is it downright somthing" (see also Nos. 342–5, 384, 449, 488).

Bayle and Berkeley both discuss the two geometrical "sophisms" which were supposed to prove the reality of the mathematical point; these are Leibniz's "sophism" of the side and the diagonal, referred to by Berkeley in entry No. 259, and that of concentric circles, mentioned by Berkeley in entry No. 315. If perpendiculars are drawn from the side of the square so as to cut the diagonal, then there is a point on the diagonal for every point on the side, and if these lines consist of points, then side and diagonal are equal, though they are seen and known to be unequal. A similar point-to-point correspondence can be established for concentric circles of different sizes.

Again, both Bayle and Berkeley trace to abstraction the mistakes of the mathematicians about composition. Bayle finds that all the alleged mathematical properties of circles, squares and other figures are based on lines without breadth, which are mere abstractions. Similarly Berkeley (No. 85) speaks of "lengths abstract from breadths [which] are the work of the mind, such do intersect in a point at all angles"; and in Nos. 391–3 he ridicules insensible sensations, insensible extensions and insensible lines, e.g. points without magnitude, lines without breadth and surfaces without colour.

After liquidating the mathematical point (*et hoc genus omne*) and the traditional atom, Bayle turns the search-light on the infinitely divisible part. Almost all contemporary thinkers supported it. Malebranche, Cheyne, Barrow, Keill, Raphson and Newton—all named in Berkeley's notebooks—all defended matter or space composed of infinitely divisible parts. Those who defend infinite divisibility, says Bayle, have the stronger case in theory; but even they cannot prove that a space millions of times less than a minute part of a barley-corn, contains an infinite number of extended parts. Berkeley takes up exactly the same position, appealing, as we now say, from theory to strong common sense. He saw clearly the crucial character of the problem; he refers to it no less than six times on the first two pages of the *Commentaries*, and in all there are some twenty entries about it.*

In his *Essay on Vision*, section 54, Berkeley puts his position about it in a nutshell: "Whatever may be said of extension in abstract, it is certain that sensible extension is not infinitely divisible." In the *Principles* sections 123–34 he goes into the question thoroughly: the infinite divisibility of finite extension is "everywhere supposed" in mathematics; mathematicians never doubt of it or question it; it is the source of geometrical paradoxes and of the extreme subtlety of mathematics; it conflicts with the principle, *esse est percipi*; for the supposed innumerable parts of a finite extension *ex hypothesi* cannot be per-

* See my note on No. 11 in the *editio diplomatica*.

ceived; a finite quantity consisting of infinite parts is a manifest contradiction; it is contrary to common sense, and it stems from the cult of abstract general ideas; there are no such things as parts infinitely small or infinitely numerous parts contained in any finite quantity.

It is remarkable that a young man of twenty-three or so could see so clearly all these aspects of a subtle and complex problem, and could write about them so confidently and accurately in the teeth of such a weight of authority. Could he have done so, one wonders, without the support of Bayle's clear thinking and plain speaking?

The main items of Berkeley's debt to his authorities may be summarized as follows: to Locke he owed his general philosophical training, his ideist terminology and his love of plain English; to Malebranche he owed the immaterial hypothesis, his interest in the philosophy of vision and the conception of all things in God; to Bayle he owed his sense of the danger of scepticism, his knowledge of Foucher's assimilation of the primary and secondary qualities, his study of the composition of extension, and his eventual rejection of mathematical points, supposed real, and of the infinite divisibility of time and space.

CHAPTER V

THE FIRST ARGUINGS

LOCKE's revision of his *magnum opus* was spread over nineteen years; Berkeley's revision was virtually complete within fifteen months. Locke's first arguings have survived, and we can see that his *Essay* opened from the original thesis, like blossom from bud. Berkeley's first arguings, as such, have not survived; but we can reconstruct their outline, and can see that the *Principles* had to be hammered into shape as the result of a catastrophic change of mind and a re-casting of basic doctrine.

The case for understanding Berkeley's phrase "my first arguings" as covering a written document or written documents, was stated above (pp. 46 ff.) in outline. In the present chapter I must fill in the details of the case with particular attention to the first two pages of the *Commentaries* and their doctrinal contents. I shall try to determine both what the first arguings did contain, and did not contain, in the hope of providing a definite background for the build-up of Berkeley's second thoughts on those deep problems with which our subsequent chapters are occupied. We are not guessing the contents of the first arguings; we are studying with a microscope the author's comments on them, and we are working back to them, as the fisheries' expert works back from the markings on the scales of the mature and travelled salmon to its early days as a fingerling in the running brook.

In this reconstruction of a lost document the first two pages of notebook B hold a key position; for on them Berkeley has written out in short pithy sentences key portions of his previous studies or comments on them, as a prelude to the revision and his later studies.

The first sixteen entries deal with eternity and time and immortality, with duration, with the succession of ideas, and with

infinite divisibility. The note on time as the succession of ideas
(No. 4), existing only in the mind (No. 13), i.e. not outside as
well, as Newton taught, together with the three entries (Nos. 8,
10, 11) on the infinite divisibility of time and space, show that
Berkeley's work on time was part and parcel of his work on
immaterialism.

Immediately after the entries on time comes a group of eight
entries (Nos. 17–24) which I take to be Berkeley's epitome of
his first arguings on matter. They are:

M   *ffall of Adam, rise of Idolatry, rise of Epicurism &
Hobbism dispute about divisibility of matter &c
expounded by material substances.*

(No. 17)

×   *Extension a sensation, therefore not without the mind.*
(No. 18)

M   *In ye immaterial hypothesis the wall is white, fire hot etc.*
(No. 19)

P   *Primary ideas prov'd not to exist in matter, after the
same manner yt secondary ones are provd not to exist
therein.*

(No. 20)

×   *Demonstrations of the infinite divisibility of extension
suppose length without breadth or invisible length wch is
absurd.*

(No. 21)

M   *World wthout thought is nec quid nec quantum nec
quale etc.*

(No. 22)

M   *'tis wondrous to contemplate ye world empty'd of
intelligences.*

(No. 23)

+ *Nothing properly but persons i.e. conscious things do exist, all other things are not so much existences as manners of ye existence of persons.*

(No. 24)

These eight entries in subject matter stand apart from the preceding entries on time, and from those on particular problems that come after. They have a broad sweep, and are not argued. They ask no questions directly. They are all on the immaterial hypothesis, and they look to me like headings or summaries for discussion. If I am not mistaken, they are the main conclusions of Berkeley's first arguings about matter, set down here for examination and revision.

The first of the group (No. 17) is a quaint jumble of topics. What have Hobbes and Epicurus to do with idolatry and Adam's Fall? What have any of them to do with material substances? They are evils, or things regarded as evils, which Berkeley's fertile imagination has lumped together with a view, no doubt, to represent the belief in matter as the original sin of intellect in the Preface or Introduction of the *Principles*. The entry has in fact left its mark on the *Principles*; for in sections 92–5 the errors of atheists, Epicureans and Hobbesists, together with idolatry, are traced to materialism.

There follow four entries which, respectively, set forth four essentials in an immaterialist theory of sense-perception. These essentials are:

(a) Extension is a sensation; therefore it is not outside the mind in matter. (No. 18)

(b) The secondary qualities are in the things of sense, and therefore not in matter. (No. 19)

(c) The same holds of the primary qualities.

(No. 20)

(d) Demonstrations of the infinite divisibility of matter proceed on the absurd supposition of real lines without breadth, and therefore invisible. (No. 21)

F

Then come three purely reflective entries, quite without argument; as if Berkeley, "on a peak in Darien," were opening the inner eye, and trying to contemplate, first, a world of matter without mind (Nos. 22, 23) and, second, a world of mind without matter (No. 24).

What would it be like? Can I envisage it?—this world of matter, this world without mind, of which they speak. What would it be? Can I assign any meaning to "a world emptied of intelligences"? It would be a string of three negations, neither fish, nor fowl, nor good red herring; it would not fall under any of the basic categories; it would be neither thing, nor quantity, nor quality; it would be "something we know not what", wondrously like *nothing*.

Then we come to the most remarkable entry in the *Commentaries*, which gives Berkeley's (1707) bird's eye view of the world without matter (No. 24). It is a daring speculative flight by a keen young thinker, who at the bidding of reason (as he saw it then) is ready to annihilate all that's made into persons and modes of personal being.

This entry ought to have drawn attention to the true nature of the *Commentaries* and the true teaching of the *Principles* and the essence of the making of the *Principles*. It has never done so yet, so far as I know. Once one has noticed it and weighed its words, and noticed the obelus set against it in the margin,* one could never rest content with the traditional mentalist account of Berkeley's teaching.

Dr. G. A. Johnston who first published the entries in *roughly* the right order, noticed this entry nearly forty years ago. He noticed *it*, and its eagle flight and bold utterance, but he did not notice the obelus. The marginal signs were not noticed or printed, much less understood in those days. Johnston made this entry the zenith of Berkeley's doctrinal development; he equated it with the discovery of the New Principle; he called it "the kernel of Berkeley's theory of knowledge and existence", and stated that Berkeley's doctrinal evolution "is complete in

* See the frontispiece, lines 17–19.

the first page" of the manuscript.* I differ profoundly. With all respect I must say that, in my opinion, Johnston misunderstood this entry and its position in Berkeley's doctrinal development. Development is "writ large" over the *whole* of the *Commentaries*, and Johnston's notion of a development of doctrine complete on its first page is too paradoxical to stand. The entry contains no hint of Berkeley's New Principle; on the contrary it is the expression and embodiment of his old Principle. The entry is the doctrinal nadir, and not the zenith; it is not the kernel of Berkeley's published philosophy, but a discarded husk. If the evolution of Berkeley's doctrine were complete on the first page, as Johnston says, of the *Commentaries*, the *raison d'être* of both the notebooks were well-nigh gone. In subsequent chapters that deal with the whole ground covered by both notebooks, we shall see the evolution of many new doctrines, and towards the end (then, and not till then) we shall witness a complete re-orientation of the original thesis. This entry may well represent the zenith of Berkeley's *first* arguings; it was the climax of his *un-revised* immaterialism; it was thus the *starting-point* of the revision and of his true line of development, and not their terminus.

What would the world be without matter? Berkeley answered, It would be a world of conscious things and modes of consciousness. That was his picture of the universe at the outset of his revision in the summer of 1707. He had resolved all reality into an ether of consciousness. His chair and table, his books and notebooks, the College park, the mountains, the great globe, and the boundless regions of space unvisited, they are all mind, and mind is all that is. The picture is clear and sharp in outline; the statement is bald and unambiguous. There is no way round it. Berkeley is not arguing upon the principles of others; he is not arguing hypothetically. He is stating his own opinion *at that time*. He states it positively and negatively; nothing exists but persons or conscious things; all other things are modes of consciousness, manners of the existence of persons.

* G. A. Johnston, *The Development of Berkeley's Philosophy* (London, 1923), p. 26.

The origin of this entry, and of the world picture it expresses, baffles those who would find all Berkeley latent in Locke; to those who study the influence of Malebranche it is as clear as daylight; for Malebranche habitually asserts that the sensible qualities are modifications of the soul, and in his excursus on the existence of bodies, discussed above (p. 64), he expressly says that reason, apart from religious faith, does not require us to believe in the existence of anything except God and our own souls. Berkeley is only putting Malebranche into his own words when he writes that nothing exists but persons and that all other things are manners of the existence of persons.

The entries in the *Commentaries*, especially those at the beginning of notebook B, are too weighty, too connected and too well orientated to be casual jottings. Nor are they the work of a novice feeling his way about a freak hypothesis for the first time, and scribbling a string of undigested comments as they come into his head. Berkeley had arranged his thoughts on these topics long before he put pen to this paper. These entries are the work of a thinker with a sure and practised touch, who is conversant with his theme, who has thought out its ramifications, who has travelled the road before and knows where it leads. In particular these eight entries (Nos. 17–24), comprehensive and penetrating and in part divergent from Berkeley's published views, have a special claim on our close attention; they form the starting-point of the revision. They are clearly the work of a serious student with a weighty thesis who has long chewed the cud of reflection. He is not satisfied with his thesis; but he cannot give it up; it will not let him go. He has hold of something; but it is not the right thing. In his dilemma he remembers the "angelic rules" of method; he sits down at his study table with a notebook open before him; he will consider anew the immaterial hypothesis; calmly and critically he will examine and revise his front-line argument. In these eight wide-ranging entries he has set out his main initial problems in abridged form, I believe, preparing them for critical analysis, as the man of science prepares his slides for the microscope.

A draft of the *Essay on Vision* was the third main component of the first arguings. An offshoot from the immaterial hypothesis and supplementary to it, the *Essay on Vision* had a definite aim and was sighted for a definite objection; it had to establish a pre-condition of immaterialism; it had to answer the materialist's objection that we see things outside the mind in space. It sought to establish that the things we actually see are in the mind, and not in space, supposed external. The nature of extension was the crux; on the one hand there was the infinitely divisible extension with which the mathematicians worked and which they claimed as real; and on the other hand there was the purely visual space from which the blind were "quite shut out", and which the Molyneux problem had brought to the front. The earlier part of notebook B is largely taken up with this pair of problems, starting with the entries:

✗   *Infinite divisibility of extension does suppose ye external existence of extension but the later is false, ergo ye former also.*

(No. 26)

✗³   *Qu: Blind man made to see would he know motion at 1st sight.*

(No. 27)

It will be noticed that the marginal sign of No. 27 refers the entry to the third main division of the *Essay on Vision*, viz. that on the heterogeneity of sight and touch. It was shown above (p. 49) that the draft *Essay* as it was in the first arguings was structurally identical with the published *Essay on Vision* except for two large portions of the work. The sections (122 ff.) on abstract ideas were not represented in the first arguings; for the attack on abstraction did not open till considerably later. Probably, too, the sections on the inverted retinal image (88–120) had no counterpart in the first arguings; for they involved a modification of the original plan of the book.

As to Berkeley's day-to-day use of the first arguings when

carrying out his revision of 1707–8, we may fairly infer that he deliberately went about from topic to topic, like a bee in a border of flowers. In his "long and scrupulous inquiry" he was determined to keep up with every aspect of his complex problem, and a careful, sympathetic reader of the notebooks can almost feel the alternating rhythm of attention. Berkeley was a hard worker and a calculating and methodical worker. Let me refer to the facts given above (p. 45) about the Draft Introduction; every day for about five weeks he did a short piece of it which would not have taken more than an hour or so. He must have been deliberately varying his study of abstract ideas with other parts of his extensive labours.

The unrevised immaterialism of Berkeley's first arguings was, it would seem, a comparatively simple theory, though quite unworkable. One of the two traditional substances was dropped, and the other left standing alone. Matter was eliminated, and only God and the soul or person remained. All the qualities of body, primary and secondary alike, were mentalized. The things we see and touch, and commonly regard as external became internal; they became modes of consciousness, modes of personal being; in feeling their "outness" we are feeling their givenness; we become aware of their Cause and of the powers He exerts on our minds. What we call *bodies* are these powers; they are intermittent; *qua* bodies they pass in and out of existence with every turn of man's attention; the perceived object is intermittent; the perceiving subject is intermittent, too, and its identity a problem.

When Berkeley returned to his thesis in the summer of 1707, with the Fellowship examination behind him and his academic career secure, he found his previous work unsatisfactory. His major premise was non-proven. Still convinced of the non-existence of matter, he knew he had not proved it. The subjectivity of the sensible qualities had furnished him with evidence, but the evidence fell short of proof; it made immaterialism look probable; it proved that we do not know by sense what matter is, or what is matter; it did not prove that matter *non est*.

And he had in the meantime read Bayle to good purpose; he saw Bayle revelling in subjectivity and relativity and the teaching of Malebranche. Berkeley became convinced of the sceptical tendencies of his own first arguings. He was soon to see that intermittency conflicted with common sense, that his conception of bodies as powers in God was untenable, that he had thought away God's world and had nothing to put in its place.

To sum up, Berkeley's first arguings, i.e. his metaphysical writings before he began his revision of 1707–8, consisted of a study of time, of the space of vision, and of the nature of sense perception in the immaterial hypothesis. These writings were all immaterialist; but they represent an immaterialism different from that of his published works. The immaterialism of Berkeley's first arguings

(1) was acosmist, i.e. it denied the real existence of body and the world of sense, as well as material substance,

(2) was not supported by the Principle, *esse est percipi*, or by the rejection of abstract general ideas,

(3) based its perceptual theory on Locke's ideism, accepting his doctrines of simple ideas, of powers (in part), and of primary and secondary qualities,

(4) based the denial of the existence of matter on the subjectivity of the sensible qualities,

(5) taught the intermittent existence of percept and of perceiver,

(6) conceived mind in terms of person and consciousness,

(7) was panpsychist, teaching that (properly speaking) only God and conscious things exist.

CHAPTER VI

THE DISCOVERY OF THE PRINCIPLE

THE making of Berkeley's philosophy was its re-making. We are now to watch the emergence of the constituent doctrines of his *revised* immaterialism. The discovery of the Principle, *esse est percipi*, came first in time and in order of importance. It was the turning-point; all hinged on it. The discovery restored Berkeley's self-confidence, and, like an injection, gave new life to his thought. It was a *discovery*, not a development; and the discoverer named it "the Principle", because it was far more to him than a new notion with a Latin formula; he saw it as a creative principle, pulsing with life, like Aaron's rod that budded. It gave a new direction to his thought about the external world, and furnished a new basis for the immaterial hypothesis.

Berkeley made the discovery, formulated it, and realised its *obviousness* or intuitive certainty about the time he made the following entries:

MP   *ffrom Malbranch, Locke & my first arguings it cant be prov'd that extension is not in matter ffrom Lockes arguings it can't be prov'd that Colours, are not in Bodies.*

(No. 265)

Mem: that I was distrustful ["sceptical", prima manu] at 8 years old and Consequently by nature disposed for these new Doctrines.

(No. 266)

M.P.   *Allowing extensions to exist in matter, we cannot know even their proportions Contrary to Malbranch.*

(No. 269)

M   *I wonder how men cannot see a truth so obvious, as that extension cannot exist without a thinking substance.*

(No. 270)

M   *I wonder not at my sagacity in discovering the obvious tho' amazing truth, I rather wonder at my stupid inadvertency in not finding it out before . . .*

(No. 279)

Emotion of any sort is rare in the notebooks; but on the three consecutive pages from which the above notes are taken, the prior anxiety and subsequent relief, and the half-suppressed joy and wonder of discovery are plain for all to see. Something decisive has occurred.

The first of these five entries (No. 265), discussed above (p. 46) for its literary implications, looks like a parting of doctrinal ways. Berkeley is taking stock; he is looking back and looking ahead. The marginal letters "MP" show that he is reviewing his old principle for disproving the existence of matter, viz. the subjectivity of the primary and secondary qualities of body. He has placed that principle in the balances and has found it wanting.

The young philosopher has come to the end of his *cul de sac*, and can go no further. His old principle has failed him. Malebranche has failed him. Locke has failed him. For years he has been trying to prove the non-existence of matter along Cartesian lines, and has constructed a philosophy on that basis. He is not satisfied with the philosophy or its basis. He has been landed in paradox and estranged from common sense, and he has found no proof of his basic principle. He is beginning to suspect that he is on the wrong tack. He has tried to demonstrate the non-existence of matter from the nature of body and its constituent qualities, and now he confides to his notebook that it "can't be proved" thus. Malebranche by design had made the existence of matter appear problematical; he had subjectified some sensible qualities and made them modes of mind. Locke had partially endorsed that attitude; he had brought the secondary qualities within the mind, and cast doubts on the real existence of the world of sense. Berkeley's authorities and his own first arguings had brought him a certain distance, and then had left him high and dry. Simon Foucher (see above p. 71) had simplified the perceptual problem and had strengthened the case for immaterialism. Where the colour is, there must the extension of the colour be. The assimilation of the primary and secondary qualities was a great step forward; but even so Berkeley was not satisfied. He could now prove that we do not know by sense that matter is, nor what it is; but he had not proved that there is no matter; and until he had laid that rock foundation, he might (for aught he could tell) be building his house upon the sand.

More is implied in this entry (No. 265) than is said. These are not the words of a beaten man. If Berkeley had not already come on a new principle, would he have troubled to record this judgment on his old principle? I think not. He would have closed the notebook, and gone off on something else, like a research student who has finally reached a *nil* result. Berkeley is clearly on tip-toe here; he is passing judgment on the old from the standpoint of the new. He is within sight of his Principle. He has made his discovery, or at least the light from it is now breaking.

The next little entry (No. 266) proves it. Here is one of the personal touches that add sauce and relish to the solid fare of these notebooks. In reflective mood Berkeley sees again Dysert Castle on the banks of the silver Nore, where he spent his childhood; some incident came back to him; perhaps even at eight years old he wondered whether its great square tower, still standing, *was* the small round object he saw far off from a bend of the Thomastown road. Even then, he remembers, he was "sceptical", questioning, distrustful of tradition, disposed by nature *for these new doctrines*.

After two entries on subsidiary problems, infinite divisibility (No. 267) and the retinal image (No. 268), Berkeley returns to the main issue, the existence of matter, in the compressed and difficult entry (No. 269), quoted in full above. Note the "M.P." in the margin. It is the end of the attempt to disprove the exist- ence of matter by internalizing the primary and secondary qualities; it represents the last kick of the old principle before the full acceptance of the new.

If extensions are in matter, Berkeley says, "we cannot know even their proportions Contrary to Malbranch". Their "pro- portions" means their size relative to our bodies. In the sixth chapter of the first book of the *Recherche* (Berkeley mentions the chapter twice, Nos. 255, 257) Malebranche tries to make good his distinction between absolute extension and relative. He says that in the case of bodies near us we know "exactly enough" their relation to our own bodies; but that as the bodies recede and their distance from us grows greater, their absolute or real size matters less and less to us, and we know less and less about it. There is a radical inconsistency here, as Berkeley saw. Malebranche is trying to have it both ways; he recognizes sense-given information about relative magnitude; he recog- nizes external bodies as large or small in proportion to our bodies; he sees it as a matter of biological necessity. How then can he turn round and postulate absolute extension, extension existing in matter out of all relation to mind?

Berkeley argues that Malebranche is wrong on the point, be- cause if extension did exist outside the mind in matter, we should not know whether things were large or small in relation to our bodies, and he implies that since we do know the relative size of things, extension is not outside the mind in matter. The significance of the argument here is that it is virtually an appeal to the New Principle; it is an appeal to the nature and meaning of *existence* as applied to extended things. When Berkeley chal- lenged the distinction between absolute and relative extension, and wrote "Contrary to Malbranch", he had reached the heart of the question. If absolute extensions exist, we could not see or touch them; nor could what we see and touch bear any pro- portion to them. When we say that extensions exist, we mean that they exist to be seen or touched. Invisible intangible

extensions are contradictions. Then like a sunburst the obviousness of it dawns on Berkeley and in No. 270 he pens his first
clear statement of the intuitive character of his Principle as
applied to extension. It has now become to him an obvious
truth that extension cannot exist without a thinking substance.
On the next page the Principle is asserted (No. 279) with even
more emphasis and without limitation to extension. It is "the
obvious tho' amazing truth" that he ought to have discovered
sooner.

The discovery of the Principle divides the revision into two
parts or periods, roughly corresponding to the two notebooks.
The discovery was the climax of notebook B, and the discovered
Principle became the starting-point of notebook A. Berkeley
made the discovery in the autumn of 1707, when he was two-
thirds of the way through notebook B. In the latter part of that
notebook he traced some of the consequences of the Principle,
and furnished it with an elaborate "demonstration" (Nos.
378–9). Then satisfied that the Principle was sound and
was capable of demonstration, he opened another notebook in
which from the first page the Principle and its corollary, the
attack on abstract general ideas, hold a commanding position.*
Under their control Berkeley's revised doctrine was worked out
in detail.

The Principle is first mentioned by that name in No. 285, and
its discovery is there attributed to his "ignorance in some sort".
I have given above (p. 73) the probable explanation of the epi-
gram. Berkeley was proud of his discovery, and any sort of
ignorance that did contribute was *docta ignorantia*. The Principle
is mentioned again by that name in Nos. 291, 304, 363, 378–9,
402, 407, 410, 411; it is often referred to elsewhere in the notebooks, and also in the published works. The Principle has various aspects and facets; it is an affirmation, a negation, a statement about the universe, and a statement about the meaning
of a term. Berkeley used it for several purposes and formulated

---

* Nos. 401, 402. On the attack on abstract general ideas as a corollary
of the Principle, see *Principles*, section 5 and below, pp. 104 ff.

it in more ways than one. It is best known by the Latin formula, *esse est percipi*, which expresses an important part of it. Berkeley uses the Latin formula in part in No. 429 and in section 3 of the *Principles*.

The Principle was for Berkeley, first and foremost, a direct, intuitive disproof of material substance, and he soon set out to make what was obvious to him obvious to everyone, by furnishing it with the demonstration (Nos. 378–9), mentioned above. There he formulates the Principle in the words:

> *that neither our Ideas nor anything like our ideas can possibly be in an unperceiving thing.*
>
> (from No. 379)

Forecast in No. 363 the demonstration consists of nineteen connected propositions, formally stated and numbered, and divided into three groups, (*a*) Nos. 1–9, which prove, or purport to prove, that no idea is in matter, and (*b*) Nos. 10–15 and (*c*) Nos. 16–19, which offer two distinct proofs that nothing like an idea is in matter. The demonstration is faulty; it makes use of two Lockeian principles (props. 1, 2) subsequently rejected; and Berkeley decided against publishing the demonstration. After promising to demonstrate all his doctrines (No. 586) he speaks in humbler tones (No. 858). Claims to demonstration are made in the *Essay on Vision* (sections 90, 95, 121, 154); but in the *Principles* demonstration is not stressed, and sections 96 and 107 tone down earlier claims.

From the moment of its discovery the Principle was to Berkeley an *obvious* truth; and a proposition, such as Thinking it so makes it so, which by general consent is not obvious, is *not* Berkeley's Principle. Opinions differ as to what is, and is not, obvious, but a certain *prima facie* obviousness is an essential hallmark of the Principle. The discovery largely consisted in discovering its obviousness. Berkeley had toyed with the notion before he really *discovered* its truth. It had been "rolling about" at his feet, like the definition of justice in Plato's *Republic*, but he had not seen it clearly and in perspective. When he penned

Nos. 33 and 37, Berkeley had seen that extension could not exist without thought, and could not exist in a thoughtless thing; but he had not seen it then as an obvious truth, flowing, not from the particular character of extension, but from the general character of existence; for he goes on arguing about it (e.g. in Nos. 40 and 55).

The epithet "obvious" is twice used in the *Commentaries* (Nos. 270, 279) of the Principle, and Berkeley comments on his stupidity in not noticing it before. There are two remarkable applications of the same epithet in the *Principles*; in section 6 it is *near and obvious* to the mind that "all those bodies which compose the mighty frame of the world, have not any subsistence without a mind, that their being is to be perceived or known". Again in section 149 Berkeley speaks of "this great truth which lies so near and obvious to the mind", viz. the intimate presence of the divine Spirit who produces ideas and sensations in our minds. The same point is made in other words in section 3 where the Principle is mentioned in print for the first time. An *intuitive* knowledge of its truth, says Berkeley, may be obtained "by any one that shall attend to what is meant by the term *exist* when applied to sensible things".

"I had rather believe all the fables in the Legend, and the Talmud, and the Alcoran than that this universal frame is without a Mind."* There is the classical statement of the obviousness of the large-scale application of Berkeley's Principle. Did not Lord Bacon speak for us all, or almost all? Do not most philosophers and men of science who think on ultimates accept the presence of universal Mind as an obvious truth? As to homelier applications of the Principle I will only say that since Berkeley drew my attention to the point, I think it a perfectly obvious truth that when I say "the book *exists*" I mean that it is perceived, or might be. I do not see what else the term *exists* there could mean, and I should think it a redundancy to say, "I see the book, *and it exists*." For in seeing it I see it existing.

In its broad aspect Berkeley's Principle is a statement about

* Bacon, *Essays, Of Atheism*.

all that is, about the nature of the universe. This aspect is uppermost in the entries already quoted from notebook B (Nos. 270, 279, 378-9); but the Principle has a homelier aspect in which it is just a statement about the meaning of the term *exist*, especially when said of sensible things; it asserts that *exist*, said of sensible things, means *to be perceived*, that their *esse* is *percipi*. The two aspects are complementary; the one shades off into the other; but they are distinct, and the distinction is worth remembering. In notebook A the homelier aspect is prominent; on its second page Berkeley declares that the vulgar notion agrees with his "when we narrowly inspect into the meaning & definition of the word Existence" (No. 408). In Nos. 472 and 473 we meet the important reminder that the term *exist* is usually confined to actual perception, but that Berkeley applies it, too, to imagined existence. The imagined existence of sensible things becomes, by the Principle, imagined perception. Hamlet's dagger in the mind is a dagger imagined visible and tangible.

The effects of the discovery of the Principle were profound. It restored Berkeley's confidence in himself and in his thesis. It was a completely new thing in philosophy, and he had found it. It restored his confidence in his senses, and clinched the break with scepticism. It explained difficulties and problems in contemporary thought, and brought him back to a common-sense belief in a world of sensible body. Externally it has left a significant mark on the format of his notebooks. As explained above (p. 56) it introduced a new marginal letter, "E" for *Existence*. One could hardly have a more objective proof of the change of viewpoint than the fact that there are twenty-nine entries in notebook A on Existence, and none at all in notebook B. Here is one of the most remarkable and revealing:

E   *Mem: Diligently to set forth how that many of the Ancient philosophers run into so great absurditys as even to deny the existence of motion and those other things they perceiv'd actually by their senses. this sprung from their*

*not knowing wt existence was and wherein it consisted
this the source of all their Folly, 'tis on the Discovering
of the nature & meaning & import of Existence that
I chiefly insist. This puts a wide difference betwixt the
Sceptics & me. This I think wholly new. I am sure 'tis
new to me*

(No. 491)

What led to the discovery? What led this young thinker to
take the unusual step of investigating the nature and meaning
and import of existence? Most of us take existence for granted,
as we take the air we breathe. *We* exist for our allotted span.
The things around us, small and great, exist; they come into
existence and pass out. Philosophers and divines discuss the
existence of God and the soul and the world; and few of us stop
to ask the nature of existence and the meaning of the term.
What put this young man of twenty-two on to the question?
What made him take down his lexicons, Hebrew and Greek,
and look up the Hebrew and Greek equivalents of the term
exist, and record them in his notebook (Nos. 412, 413)?

It was not Locke's doing. Locke classed *existence* with *unity* as
simple ideas "that are suggested to the understanding by every
object without and every idea within"; he discussed our knowledge of the existence of God, of the self, of spirits and of other
things, and he graded that knowledge.* He equated *to exist* and
to be; but if I am not mistaken, he did not examine critically the
meaning of either verb. Berkeley claimed at any rate to have
thought it out for himself, and thought his answer "wholly
new".

In his study of extension or space, particularly in his study of
the mathematical theories of its composition, Berkeley's attention was called to the meaning of the term *exist*; in those fields
the nature of existence and the meaning of the term became
problems to him; and the discovery of the Principle followed.

The immaterial hypothesis was bound up with the meta-

* Locke, *Essay*, II, vii, 7, and IV, ix–xi.

physics of space. Philosophers commonly associate space and matter, and French philosophy in Berkeley's day almost identified them. Berkeley's interest in the nature of space was full and varied.* For his *Essay on Vision* he had to study the relation between the space of sight and the space of touch. He had to relate both to the space of geometry, and consider together abstract space and sensible space. The recent discovery of fluxions and the calculus had intensified the mathematicians' long-standing interest in the composition of space, and Berkeley was deeply concerned with the *pros* and *cons* of infinite divisibility; for if it is true, as almost all philosophers and mathematicians of Berkeley's day held that space is composed of real parts, infinitely divisible into real parts, then there is a dark spot in every drop of water and every grain of sand, and the existence of matter cannot be disproved.

Does space exist in matter? That is the central question of the first half of notebook B. It was shadowed by a supplemental question, viz. Does anything like space exist in matter? When he was penning the early entries, his reply to both questions would have been, "I think, *Not*; but I cannot prove it." Take, for instance, the following entry:

M   *If a piece of matter have extension yt must be determin'd to a particular bigness & figure, but etc.*

(No. 40)

When he wrote those words, it was not *obvious* to him that extension was not in matter; he is feeling his way towards it, but he had not yet reached intuitive certainty; his argument is indirect, complex and demonstrative. Filled out, it would have run as follows: If a piece of matter has extension, it must have a particular size and shape; but size and shape are the work of the mind and are relative to mind; the size of a small salmon is

---

* In all 302 entries have the marginal sign X, which is, no doubt, the "Ex–" of *Extension*. Those with numbers refer to visual and tangible space; those without numbers mostly refer to mathematical space; and the usage was, I think, extended to cover mathematics in general.

G

the size of a large trout; the shape of Dysert Castle is square from here, round from there. If then we attribute size and shape to our piece of matter, *eo ipso* we attribute to it intrinsic relation to mind; we are supposing a piece of matter conditioned by mind; we are supposing a contradiction, viz. matter that is not matter—which is absurd. Berkeley's argument at that stage was *ad absurdum* and roundabout; it became intuitive and direct when he reached the Principle. From the standpoint of the Principle you look at the space of the astronaut, or at the space of his back garden, and you see at once that those spaces are in necessary relation to mind.

But to return to our original supposition (No. 40). It is very hard to suppose a piece of matter round or square, a yard long and a foot high, hard or soft, and with the other features of visible and tangible space. It seems better to suppose that matter has qualities *like* those of sense, but not identical with them. This supposition keeps our world of sense in touch with material reality without identifying them. It works out in the theory that we see and touch copies or resemblances of material reality, and gives rise to the supplemental question, formulated above, Does anything like space exist in matter?

As with the main question, Berkeley's early handling of this supplemental question is tentative and unsure. Consider, for example, the following entries:

M   *Qu: wt can be like a sensation but a sensation?*

(No. 46)

Qu: Did ever any man see any other things besides his own ideas, that he should compare them to these & make these like unto them?

(No. 47, cf. No. 51)

Here Berkeley argues from the psychological impossibility of comparing what is in the mind, e.g. colour, with what *ex hypothesi* is outside the mind in matter. A little later, arguing upon the principles of others, he introduces a new and effective point:

M   *Our ideas we call figure & extension not images of the
        figure & extension of matter, these (if such there be)
        being infinitely divisible, those not so.*

                                                (No. 81)

Here Berkeley summons infinite divisibility to his aid. Even if
you could compare them, he says in effect, you would find no
likeness; the objects compared are basically *unlike*; for sensible
shape and size are not infinitely divisible; whereas material
shape and size, *ex hypothesi* are infinitely divisible.

In the "demonstration" of the Principle towards the end of
the notebook, the *likeness* question has two sections to itself, and
in both of them the same conclusion is drawn, viz.:

        Nothing like an idea can be in an unperceiving thing.
                                        (No. 378, 15, 19)

But now watch the assurance and incisiveness of his treatment
at the end of the *Commentaries* a year or so later, when he has
fully absorbed the intuitive argument. The *likeness* theory gets
short shrift:

M.   *Is it not nonsense to say a Smell is like a thing wch
        cannot be smelt, a Colour is like a thing which cannot
        be seen.*

                                                (No. 862)

Does space exist in matter? Does anything like space exist in
matter? In seeking and finding his answers to both those questions Berkeley discovered his Principle. His notebooks show that
in both cases his style of argument altered. It began as an
indirect argument from consequences; it began as *demonstrative*,
as Locke would say. It ended as direct and *intuitive*. Berkeley
came to see it as *obvious* that neither space nor anything like
space can exist in matter. This "obvious truth" was forced on
him by his long course of study of space and, particularly, of the
composition of space. He had to examine microscopically the
nature of space; he had to compare and contrast competing

types of space. He had repeatedly to ask himself the question, What does the term *exist* mean when said of this space or that? In this way Berkeley's attention was turned to the nature of *existence*, and to the meaning of that term. In this way the question of existence arose, took root in his mind, flowered in his Principle, and changed his tentative and timorous handling of basic problems in notebook B into the firm grasp and magisterial assurance shown in notebook A and the *Principles*.

There are in the *Commentaries* scores and scores of entries on incommensurability and other mathematical topics that at first sight have nothing to do with immaterialism. They are all germane; they are part and parcel of Berkeley's study of space, and many of them bear directly on the crucial question of the infinite divisibility of space. Some thirty entries deal explicitly with infinite divisibility, and all but two of them occur in notebook B. That is a significant fact. Infinite divisibility was an important issue to Berkeley when he was casting about for a disproof of the existence of matter; but it ceased to trouble him once he had discovered the Principle and settled the main lines and character of his immaterialism. In the *Principles*, sections 123–32 he deals at some length with infinite divisibility; it is one of the false principles, he says, that give rise to geometrical paradoxes, repugnant to common sense, and the geometrical arguments for it are "bottomed", he says, on the doctrines of the external existence of the objects of sense and of abstract general ideas.

Leaning heavily on Bayle's article *Zeno** Berkeley went very thoroughly into those geometrical arguments. He faced the "Difficulties about Concentric Circles" (No. 315); two circles with a common centre are unequal; they can be shown to be equal by drawing a geometrical figure which gives a one–one correspondence between the points of the circles. The argument is valid only on the assumption that circles are literally composed of mathematical points. Leibniz's "sophism" to prove the side of the square equal to the diagonal illustrates the same

* See above, p. 74.

assumption (No. 259). Scores of entries contrast mathematical points with Berkeley's own sensible *minima*. His *minima* have magnitude and make up sensible lines and sensible surfaces. Mathematical points have no magnitude; they are "nothings". Berkeley studied the angle of contact (Nos. 168, 309, 381) in which the calculus originated in part; he studied incommensurability, surds and the doubling of the cube (Nos. 258, 263, 306, 469, 482); he observed J. Keill in his *Introductio ad veram physicam* (1702), "filling the world with a mite" (No. 364). Now all these geometrical problems, theorems and sophisms, discussed on page after page of the notebooks, hinge on the composition of space and the figures of space, and they set the space of geometry and the space of sight and touch in stark contrast. The geometrician has to work with points that have no magnitude, points that are invisible and insensible; he has to work with lines, without breadth, without colour, lines that are invisible and insensible. Berkeley and Bayle held that such points and lines are not those of real life. Sentient creatures in real life, as distinct from abstract thought, need sensible points and lines; we have to work with points and lines that we can see and touch. The game of cricket requires a popping-crease composed of white lines of considerable breadth; bowling and batting under M.C.C. rules could not take place without them. The axioms of geometry must not be shaken; but cricket must go on!

The problem of infinite divisibility forced a decision. Berkeley had to make up his mind. He had to choose between abstractions and realities. He had to choose between points with magnitude and points with position alone, between visible lines with breadth and invisible lines without. His decision is registered on the second page of notebook B where he wrote:

✗   *Demonstrations of the infinite divisibility of extension suppose length without breadth or invisible length wch is absurd.*

(No. 21, cf. 342)

In this context the question of existence would inevitably arise. Are they real? Do they exist? In what sense do they exist? What does *exist* mean? Such is the existential catechism. The lines and points I see *exist*. I could not see them, if they did not exist; and just because I can *see* them, I say they *exist*. The mathematician works with *his* lines and points; in some sense they exist; but their existence is not real existence; it is not the existence of the lines and points I see. The mathematician sees them with his mind's eye, as we can see a gold mountain with the mind's eye. He imagines they exist; and in a large sense they may be said to exist, just because they are imagined visible. I use the word Existence, says Berkeley, "in a larger sense than ordinary", i.e. not confining it to "actual perception".*

The mathematical problems of the composition of space turn the search-light on existence, and spot-light the issue. We can think of a real line that cannot be seen by Socrates from here; we cannot think of a real line that cannot be seen by any one from any where. Lines absolutely invisible and intangible are not real; they do not exist. The same holds of points and surfaces. It holds of triangles and circles and all other figures of space, and of space in the large. Whenever we attribute real existence to space or to any mode of space, *eo ipso* we attribute to it actual or possible relation to mind. If we can attain that insight, as Berkeley held he did when he discovered the Principle, it then becomes *obvious* that space does not exist in matter, and that nothing like space exists in matter. From that generalization about space it is a short step to the Principle, which was Berkeley's distinctive discovery, viz. that the predicate *exist* by its very import and meaning brings all reality within the range and orbit of mind, perceiving or imagining or conceiving.

* Nos. 472–3. See below, p. 148, and compare *Principles*, section 23, where imagined existence is shown to be imagined perception.

CHAPTER VII

ABSTRACT GENERAL IDEAS

FROM the account given above (p. 45) of Berkeley's early writings the reader will see that in the making of his doctrine of abstraction a third notebook, the Chapman manuscript, played an important part. It stands midway between the *Commentaries* and the published Introduction to the *Principles*. Its chief content is known as "the draft Introduction",* which is considerably longer than the published Introduction; by cutting it down Berkeley has left some points obscure, notably that about words as a cause of abstract general ideas; a reference to the draft clears up these obscurities. The draft embodies several entries from the *Commentaries*, which have disappeared from the published work; of special importance are those that concern the experimental conceit of "the Solitary Man". The draft shows the close and careful use Berkeley made of the *Commentaries* in his revising work, and as almost every paragraph is dated to a day, it facilitates the task of tracing accurately the development of Berkeley's thought.

The Introduction on abstract general ideas, in its published form as well as in the draft, was in the main an afterthought, due to Berkeley's discovery of the Principle. It does not fit in well with the body of the work; for it speaks the language of Locke's ideism, and gives no hint of Berkeley's specialist use of the term *idea* for the thing of sense. In its use of the terms *abstract* and *general* it is inconsistent, confused and confusing. Still, as the gateway to immaterialism, the Introduction serves its purpose well, disposing the reader to think in terms of the concrete, and warning him against the notions of existence with nothing to exist, and extension without extended content.

* The draft Introduction has been published in full by Jessop (*Works*, Vol. II, pp. 121 ff.).

The mind's tendency to false abstraction was Berkeley's second *discovery*. I take the term from Hume, who calls Berkeley's doctrine, "One of the greatest and most valuable discoveries that has been made of late years."* Berkeley himself uses the verb *discover* in describing his attempts to locate the causes of philosophical error.† It was indeed a discovery. Berkeley found it and was not taught it. We can trace its source in the *Commentaries*, and can see it coming. Hobbes and Malebranche condemn certain types of abstraction. Peter Browne, who was Provost when Berkeley was an undergraduate, has a chapter on Abstraction that has certain points in common with Berkeley;‡ his book was published in 1728, and he probably learned from Berkeley, rather than Berkeley from him. Berkeley's treatment of abstraction and its dangers is quite distinctive. No one before him handled the attack on abstract ideas so systematically; no one before him fashioned out of it such a powerful weapon.

Berkeley developed his characteristic views on abstraction while he was filling the last quarter of notebook B; they were largely the result of his discovery of the Principle. Three distinct considerations lead to that conclusion; they are (1) the position of the sections on abstraction in the *Essay on Vision*, (2) the altered plans for the Introduction to the *Principles* and (3) the doctrinal connection between the Principle and the attack on abstract general ideas. Let me explain these three points.

The argument of the *Essay on Vision* reaches its climax in section 121 with the discussion of the heterogeneity of sight and touch, and there Berkeley undertakes "to inquire more particularly concerning the difference between the ideas of sight and touch. . . ." Then abruptly and with practically no warning§ four sections (122–5) are introduced containing a full-dress attack on abstract general ideas and Locke's abstract idea of a

* Hume, *Treatise of Human Nature*, 1739, I, vii.

† *Principles*, Introduction, section 4.

‡ P. Browne, *The Procedure, Extent and Limits of Human Understanding*, pp. 186 ff.

§ In section 43 there is a casual reference to abstracting colour from extension, and in section 54 a mention of extension in abstract.

triangle. The insertion is clumsily made; the opening cue of section 122 on abstraction comes in awkwardly after the promise of the more particular inquiry into heterogeneity given in the previous section.

Once it is said, it is perfectly obvious that "when men speak of extension as being an idea common to two senses, it is with a secret supposition that we can single out extension from all other tangible and visible qualities, and form thereof an abstract idea . . . common both to sight and touch." Once it is pointed out, the application of Berkeley's doctrine of abstraction to the problem of this heterogeneity is perfectly obvious. Yet Berkeley had been working at this problem for weeks and months, if not years, without seeing the connection or writing a word about it in the appropriate part of his notebook. There are forty-five entries in the *Commentaries*, marked in the margin X³ or X³ᵃ for inclusion in the third division of the *Essay on Vision*, i.e. the heterogeneity division; and none of them mention abstraction, not even Nos. 49 and 70.

If Berkeley had views on abstraction at the earlier stages of his revision, they would have come to the surface when he was planning his treatment of the heterogeneity of (*a*) visible and tangible distance, and (*b*) visible and tangible size. But, no. Here are his plans:

✗³   *Visible distance heterogeneous from tangible distance demonstrated 3 several ways.*

✗³   *1st if a tangible inch be equal or in any other reason to a visible inch, thence it will follow yt unequals are equals wch is absurd. for at wt distance would the visible inch be placed to make it equal to the tangible inch?*

✗³   *2d One made to see yt had not yet seen his own limbs or anything he touch'd, upon sight of a foot length would know it to be a foot length if tangible foot & visible foot were the same idea, sed falsum id ergo & hoc.*

✗³   *3dly from Molyneux's problem wch otherwise is falsely
solvd by Locke & him.*

(No. 49)

✗³   *Tangible & visible extension heterogeneous because they
have no common measure: also because their simplest
constituent parts or elements are specifically distinct, viz.
punctum visible & tangibile. N.B. The former seems to
be no good reason.*

(No. 70)

Then again, the published Introduction on abstract general
ideas was not the one originally planned. When he was filling
the earlier pages of notebook B, Berkeley had other plans, viz.:

+   *Preliminary discourse about singling & abstracting
simple ideas.*

(No. 139)

+   *Mem: Introduction to contain the design of the whole
the nature & manner of demonstrating &c.*

(No. 212, cf. No. 586)

Both those entries are obelized, and the obelus must mark
substantial modifications of earlier plans; for the Introduction,
as published, makes no mention of simple ideas; it has only two
sections on demonstration (15, 16), and it has nothing on "the
design of the whole". General aims are mentioned in section 4;
but "the whole" must refer to the composite work, originally
planned, of which the *Principles* was only "Part I".* The

* The *Principles* came out as Part I in 1710; the "Part I" was omitted
from the title-page in the second edition, though retained at the beginning
of the text. Part II was lost during his travels in Italy; it dealt with spirit and
moral philosophy. Berkeley mentions it in the Preface to the *Three Dialogues*,
in his draft letter to Le Clerc (*Works*, Vol. VIII, p. 48), and in his letter to
Johnson (*Works*, Vol. II, p. 282).

In the *Commentaries* the first book is mentioned in Nos. 571, 792, the
second book, in Nos. 508, 807, 878, and the third book (on natural philosophy) in Nos. 583, 853. The *Essay on Vision* was an offshoot from "Part I",
and was not part of the original "design of the whole".

Introduction as we have it now is mentioned for the first time in No. 401.

The third consideration is the doctrinal connection between the two discoveries. If Berkeley had not discovered his Principle and the meaning of the term *exist*, abstract general ideas might never have caught his attention. The two discoveries were made in the same field—the mathematics of extension—where the second follows closely from the first. Berkeley speaks of the two principles together and says that the geometrical arguments for infinite divisibility "are bottomed on them".* Asking himself why the mathematicians stuck so stubbornly to those arguments which he and Bayle had found so unconvincing, Berkeley, as we saw above (p. 96), became aware that the meaning of the term *exist* was a problem, found his own solution, and went on to inquire why other thinkers had not found his solution, or would not accept it. False abstraction was, he decided, the reason why.

Berkeley's Principle and his attack on abstract general ideas stem from the same studies, and were both discoveries; but they are not of equal importance; for depth and consequence and insight the *esse est percipi* is the greater achievement, *pace* Hume. Berkeley's immaterialism hinges on the Principle, and cannot be understood without it; but if the Introduction had never been written, the substantial teaching of the book would not be affected. The body of the work is an account of reality as Berkeley saw it. The Introduction facilitates acceptance of that account, but otherwise contributes little. In itself the Introduction is a critical account of the mistaken principles of other thinkers. It is just what it claims to be (section 4), an attempt to discover the sources of philosophical doubt, uncertainty, absurdities and contradictions. To ignore or undervalue the Introduction would be foolish; to spend too much time on its subtleties or to allow it to obscure the main issue is to put the cart before the horse.

We have now to trace the rise and development of the

* *Principles*, section 125.

abstraction theme in the *Commentaries*. In the earlier part of note-book B there are two or three casual references to abstraction; but there is no evidence of any sustained interest in the theme. Lengths abstract from breadth and colour abstract from exten-sion are mentioned in No. 85, and the idea of a circle in abstract is denied in No. 238. An apparent exception is:

✗ *The Mob use not the word Extension tis an abstract term of the Schools.*

(No. 111a)

Here Berkeley is obviously on the scent and in full cry.* But like most of the *verso* entries this is a later comment; it echoes No. 772, and it appeals to the criterion of "The Mob". All the other references to the "mob" and the "vulgar" occur in note-book A. There are no less than ten in all—viz. Nos. 111a, 405, 544, 552, 643, 703, 724, 740, 772, 867. It is a remarkably long list, and some of the entries are very striking. "I side in all things with the Mob" (No. 405). "We must wth the Mob place certainty in the senses" (No. 740). To take such statements as paradoxes or mere literary pose is to misunderstand Berkeley and his revised immaterialism. In their context he meant them literally and seriously. We might almost call Berkeley's criterion of the mob and the vulgar his "third discovery"; and all three discoveries are mentioned together on the first page of note-book A. This was no accident; for Berkeley's intellectual return to the common sense of the common man after his involvement with continental scepticism and the "sublime notions" of Male-branche was a direct consequence of his discovery of the Principle.

Serious and sustained attention to abstraction and false abstraction begins with the query:

> *Qu. is it not impossible there shou'd be General ideas ? All ideas come from without, they are all particular. The mind, tis true, can consider one thing wthout another,*

* The hunting metaphor is his; see No. 521.

+ *but then consider'd asunder they make not 2 ideas. both together can make but one as for instance Colour & Visible extension.*

(No. 318)

After thus formally raising the question and formulating the problem Berkeley continued to study it off and on for some weeks. In Nos. 328, 362, 365, 391, 392 and 393 various false abstractions come up for review; in Nos. 342, 363a, and 365a abstraction and the Principle are considered together. Nothing strikingly new emerges; but in this period Berkeley made up his mind on the main issue, answered his own query, and recorded his decision at the head of the new notebook:

I *No general Ideas, the contrary a cause of mistake or confusion in Mathematiques etc. this to be intimated in ye Introduction.*

(No. 401)

Here mathematical studies are indicated as the source of the doctrine, and Berkeley looks forward to embodying it in his Introduction. The Principle is named in the very next entry, and it is clear that with the opening of notebook A, probably in the early winter of 1707–8, the revision of the immaterial hypothesis took a decisive turn which led straight to the doctrines of the *Principles*, guided by the principle, *esse est percipi*, and assisted by the rejection of abstract general ideas.

Before we consider further developments in the doctrine of abstraction, let us pause on the terms, *abstract*, *general* and *abstract general*. Berkeley in his books and notebooks is consistently inconsistent in using them. Perhaps he had to be; perhaps this is another instance of his dialectical method of conveying his views. At times he uses the three terms indifferently, in effect making all abstract ideas general, and all general ideas abstract. At other times he makes a sharp distinction between them, and *uses* the term *abstract* to limit *general*. Thus in section 12 of the Introduction he writes, "And here it is to be noted that I do not deny absolutely there are general ideas, but only that there are any *abstract general ideas*; for in the passages above quoted [from Locke], wherein there is mention of general ideas, it is always supposed that they are formed by *abstraction*, after the manner set forth in Sect. 8 and 9. Now if we will annex a meaning to our words, and speak only of what we can conceive, I believe we shall acknowledge, that an idea, which considered in it self is particular, becomes general, by being made to represent or stand for all other particular ideas of the same sort."

The statement looks clear and reasonable, until one probes. Does it square with the facts, and what exactly does it mean? Look back at the two crucial entries (Nos. 318, 401) quoted above. Berkeley asks, Are there general ideas? And he answers, No; there are none. The denial is absolute; *abstract* general ideas are not mentioned. When one looks more closely, and notices the obelus in the margin of No. 318, *placed low down*, a possible explanation suggests itself. Berkeley did not change his answer to the query; but he did change his reasons for the answer. Formerly (No. 318) he gave as his reasons that all ideas come from without and are all particular; on reflection he disapproves of both statements. Ideas of the imagination do not come from without, and now he feels forced to say that not all ideas are particular; for some are general.

Berkeley is *speaking* in terms of Locke's representative idea and *thinking* in terms of his own idea-thing. As a common-sense realist he accepts sorts, generals, universals; he has just mentioned "particulars of the same *sort*"; the "sorts" are there, no matter how we explain them, and in his own terminology the sorts are ideas. But at the moment he is arguing with Locke's followers; in particular he is arguing against those who held that we can and do and must (if we are to have general knowledge) form the general idea of a triangle "neither oblique nor rectangle, neither equilateral, equicrural, nor scalenon, but *all and none of these at once*."* It cannot be done, he says; we cannot and do not form *such* general ideas; and the opinion that we

* Locke, *Essay*, IV, vii, 9.

can is a root of scepticism. If Berkeley accepted Locke's general idea of a triangle, by the same token he would have to accept general ideas, similarly made, of extension in abstract, existence in abstract and matter in abstract. No wonder he viewed his attack on Locke's "absurd triangle" as "the killing blow" (No. 687). Having to argue this important case on the principles of others and with their terminology, Berkeley could hardly help some verbal inconsistency.

A further source of trouble is his own account of generality. If it is adequate to the facts, it should be expressed more carefully. He has given the impression of paying lip-service to generality, while in effect denying it. Does an idea which considered in itself is particular "become general" in any real sense by being made to stand for all other particulars of the same sort? Berkeley does not discuss this question. He is content to argue that we cannot frame and use a general idea of man or motion or matter or existence; we cannot demonstrate about it; we may think we can, as did Locke; but all we are in fact doing in such a case is to consider separately some common feature of a man, motion, etc., and ignore its particularity. In the cut and thrust of debate Berkeley takes little or no account of generality; his concern is with particulars, and his main task is to distinguish particulars, such as nose and mouth which can exist separately from particulars such as this line, this colour, this extension which cannot do so. When he puts all his cards on the table, rejects the representative idea, takes ideas of the imagination as the only ideas we *frame*, and normally means by *idea* an actual object of sense, it matters little to him whether any idea under discussion is viewed as a particular taken generally or as a general taken particularly. If, for instance, Berkeley is on his crucial question, the nature of extension, it is all-important to him that the real line—the line he sees, should not be an abstract AB without breadth, invisible, without colour; but a concrete visible object, with length and breadth and colour and two visible "ends" which, like those of Locke's pen, are black or white.

Berkeley was right to attack Locke's views on abstraction and to ridicule his lapse over the triangle; if such fictions are allowed to pass for facts, then indeed the sceptics triumph and materialism is secure. Berkeley had to attack false abstraction; but his natural target was the abstract *particular*. In his own words, "He that knows he has no other than particular ideas, will not puzzle himself in vain to find out and conceive the abstract idea . . ."* Abstract triangles, abstract points and lines and surfaces, abstract extensions and extension, abstract colours and smells and touches, abstract existents and existence— Berkeley must sweep them all away if his immaterialism is to get a hearing, and whether such objects are particulars in their particularity or particulars "become general" is irrelevant to his argument. That presumably is the explanation of his inconsistency in his use of the technical terms.

I come now to consider the entries on abstraction in notebook A. There are over thirty of them. One or two new points come up; there are new and interesting applications of the doctrine; in the doctrine itself there is little or no development, and, indeed, little room for development. The attempt to trace the source of abstraction to words gave rise to the curious conceit of "the Solitary Man", which is prominent in the *Commentaries* and in the draft, but was omitted entirely in the last stages of the revision.

Existence naturally comes in for attention; it is an abstract idea, not thought of by the vulgar; the term was coined by the schools, Nos. 552, 725, 772; it is an abstract idea in use by the Cartesians, No. 811; existence is nothing without, or distinct from, perception, and a good proof may be had by considering the Solitary Man (No. 588).

Extension apart from sensible qualities is an abstract idea, No. 440; along with existence it is dismissed as an abstract idea, i.e. no idea, unknown to the vulgar, No. 772.

In No. 873 the question is raised whether *veritas* is an abstract idea. The subject is not pursued. Another quite new application

* *Principles*, Introduction, section 24.

is made at the end of the long discussion of man's faculties, will, volition and understanding; they too are abstract ideas, not used by the vulgar, Nos. 867, 871 (cf. *Principles*, sect. 143); and the mind is "the Concrete of the Will & understanding" (No. 713).

Locke argues that the power of framing abstract ideas distinguishes man from beast. Berkeley makes a humorous reference to that argument in section 11 of the Introduction, and implies that the power of speech is the real point; Locke supposes that beasts cannot abstract and generalize because they have not the use of words, and that men can form abstract general ideas because they can speak. Berkeley makes two references to the point in the *Commentaries* (Nos. 594, 753) and suggests other *differentiae*, viz. shape, speech and imagination ("the composition of ideas").

Berkeley's feeling for polemic and for literary detail comes out in his phrase "the killing blow" (No. 687) for his exposure of Locke's absurd triangle; he will keep it for the last for the sake of effect; he does in point of fact bring it in almost "at the last" in the section on Locke's views (section 13). Perhaps he had a twinge of conscience about his attack on Locke, and the very next entry (No. 688) records his sense of "the Candour of this great man".

I will conclude this section by quoting in full two entries which reveal better than anything in the published Introduction how little Berkeley cared for the technical distinction between abstract and general, and how deeply he felt the substantial issue. His attack on abstract ideas was more than an explanation of the prevalence of materialism; it was a challenge to the "supercilious pride" of Montaigne and the continental sceptics. He has the sceptical tendencies of Locke's fourth Book in mind, too; for the phrase "sheaves and bundles" is based on Locke's *Essay*, Book IV, xii, 12. Berkeley recognized legitimate abstraction; he admitted that we can and do consider separately parts, whether they are physically separable or mentally distinguishable; but he did not accept a colour as physically

H

separable or mentally distinguishable from its spread. For Berkeley the unpardonable sin of intellect is to take the part for the whole, to separate the chip from the block and the stone from the living rock, and to substitute mental abstractions, ghosts of the departed, for the concrete realities of sense and spirit. Here are the two telling entries:

+   *Qu: How can there be any abstract ideas of Colours? it seems not so easily as of tastes or sounds. But then all abstract ideas whatsoever are particular. I can by no means conceive a general idea. 'Tis one thing to abstract one idea from another of a different kind. & another thing to abstract an idea from all particulars of the same kind.*
(No. 497)

| *These men with a supercilious Pride disdain the common single informations of sense. they grasp at Knowlege by sheaves & bundles ('tis well if catching at two [sic] much at once they hold nothing but emptyness & air). they in ye depths of their understanding Contemplate Abstract Ideas. etc Introduction*
(No. 748)

Berkeley's study of words was a direct outcome of his doctrine of abstraction. Almost all the entries on words are in the latter part of the *Commentaries*. The outcome of the study is contained principally in sections 18–25 of the Introduction; it is part and parcel of the attack on abstract ideas. There is one section (120) on words in the *Essay on Vision*: it occurs at the very spot where Berkeley introduced four sections on abstract ideas (see above p. 49). No doubt he made the two insertions at the same time. His general aim is to explode the notion that general names stand for general ideas and imply the existence of abstract general ideas. He desires to further Locke's attack on jargon and to endorse Locke's plea for a measure of wordless thought, and at the same time to torpedo Locke's principle that all significant words stand for ideas. At first, as I noticed above

(p. 61),* Berkeley accepted that principle *ex animo*; it was part of the current ideism; he made it an axiom, and placed it at the head of his "demonstration" of the Principle (No. 378); but later he learned that many important words have emotive value and little or no ideational content; and when he discovered that this "axiom" was part and parcel of Locke's argument for abstract general ideas, he rejected it. "He that knows names do not always stand for ideas will spare himself the labour of looking for ideas where there are none to be had."†

This rejection had far-reaching consequences for Berkeley's system. If Berkeley realized at the time how far it reached (which may be doubted), it was an act of daring. If all significant words do not stand for ideas, and if we are free to use words without ideational content, what of the words *God* and *soul*? In due course Berkeley learned to deny that we have ideas of God and the soul, and the denial marked an epoch in the making of his doctrine of mind and spirit, as we see below (p. 167). The denial was an act of common sense, as on reflection most thinkers must admit; if there is a God, we cannot possibly have an idea of Him; we cannot possibly form or conceive a static picture of His dynamic reality. Nor can our intimate awareness of our active spiritual selves precipitate itself into a passive idea of the soul. But these denials fly in the face of two millenniums of conservative, educated opinion. Young Berkeley took the step. Later in life he made an effective application of the same principle to the words *force* and *grace*. In a brilliant discussion in the seventh dialogue of the *Alciphron* he shows that both terms can be used without corresponding ideas; his mind goes back to his early rejection of abstraction, and he concludes (section 8) that the philosopher is not free from bias and prejudice "who shall maintain the doctrine of force and reject that of grace, who shall admit the abstract idea of a triangle, and at the same time ridicule the Holy Trinity".

In the *Commentaries* Berkeley makes Locke's account of truth

* *Essay*, III, xi, 8.
† *Principles*, Introduction 24.

his starting-point for his study of words and abstraction. He writes:

I   *Locke cannot explain general Truth or Knowlege with-*
out treating of words & propositions. This makes for
me against general Ideas—v. Locke Lib. 4: ch: 6.

(No. 555)

Truth, Locke says, consists in the joining or separating of signs according as the things signified agree or disagree; general truths need words; they have to be expressed in verbal proposi-tions, and since general propositions about substances are never certain, we can attain general knowledge only by "the contemplation of our own abstract ideas".

Locke's case is not particularly clear or cogent; but Berkeley was impressed by the fact that Locke could not deal with truth and knowledge without first treating of words, and in that fact found support for his attack on abstract ideas. In section 18 of the Introduction Berkeley traces to language the source of Locke's doctrine of abstraction, referring especially to Locke's section* on the necessity of general names to the completing and acceptance of *genera* and *species*. People think that every name ought to have one precise meaning; but since the one name has to cover a large number of particular things that differ, the one precise meaning will not be found in any one particular, and must therefore be sought in an abstract idea that covers them all. "A silent and a striking watch," says Locke, "are but one species to those who have but one name for them: but he that has the name 'watch' for one, and 'clock' for the other, and distinct complex ideas to which those names belong, to him they are different species." Berkeley goes part of the way here with Locke; he thinks that words have contributed to mistaken views on abstraction, and that taking the com-munication of ideas to be the sole function of language, and insisting, as Locke does, that all significant names stand for ideas, have made further contributions to the error; but he has

* *Essay*, III, vi, 39.

deeper instances in mind than Locke had. Berkeley is thinking of the abstraction of extension from colour, and existence from things that exist, not merely of the abstraction of the notion of a watch from that of a time-piece.

Berkeley, with Locke, assumes that speech is only the *utterance* of thought, and that doubtful assumption underlies his interesting conceit of "the Solitary Man". Having no one to talk to, the Solitary thinks silently; would he, or would he not, form abstract ideas of things? That was the question. It was more than a question to Berkeley; it was a psychological experiment. Like a Trappist monk he refrained from speaking for periods in order to test the results of wordless thought. He was on the brink of the experiment when he penned the entry:

> *If men did not use words for Ideas they would never have thought of abstract ideas. certainly genera & species are not abstract general ideas. These include a contradiction in their nature v. Locke Lib. 4 S.9.c.7.*
>
> (No. 561)

On the next page he refers to Bacon's Idols which are imposed by words on the understanding, and spring "out of a faulty and unskilful abstraction".* Then after another reference to Locke on words (No. 565) the conceit is formulated:

> *Of great use & ye last Importance to Contemplate a man put into the world alone wth admirable abilitys. & see how after long experience he would know wthout words. Such a one would never think of Genera & Species or abstract general Ideas.*
>
> (No. 566)

The conceit of the Solitary Man was an attempt to reach in thought the pure data of experience; it has points in common with the *Philosophus Autodidactus* of the Arabian tale, and with Defoe's *Robinson Crusoe* (1719) and his *Dumb Philosopher* (1719). I imagine Berkeley took the notion from Molyneux's problem

* Nov. Org. Bk. I, 59–60.

of the blind man made to see. His Solitary Man was to do for
words and ideas what Molyneux's problem had done for sight
and touch. Berkeley took it very seriously for a time; it is
applied again to abstract ideas in No. 727, to the *esse est percipi* in
No. 588, to identical propositions in No. 592, to the recording of
ideas in No. 607, to number in No. 648, and to complex ideas
in No. 727a; and when he speaks of the "marvellous emptiness
& scarcity of Ideas" of the man who will lay aside all use of
words (No. 600), it is clear that he is speaking from personal
experience, and perhaps unconsciously condemning its futility.
The experimenting may have left its mark in the conception of
the dumb men made to speak, mentioned in the third dialogue;*
otherwise it is not mentioned in the published works.

In the draft Introduction, however, it figured largely.† After
section 21 Berkeley originally wrote a long section beginning,
"Let us conceive a Solitary Man, one born and bred to such a
place of the world and in such circumstances, as he shall never
have had occasion to make use of universal signs for his ideas.
That man shall have a constant train of particular ideas passing
in his mind. Whatever he sees, hears, imagines, or any wise
conceives is on all hands, even by the patrons of abstract ideas,
granted to be particular. . . . Such a one I should take to be
nearer the discovery of certain great and excellent truths yet
unknown, than he that has had the education of the Schools. . . ."
After section 21 on the excellent use of words Berkeley continues, "I shall therefore endeavour so far as I am able to put
my self in the position of the solitary philosopher. I will confine
my thoughts and enquirys to the scene of my particular ideas,
from which I may expect to derive the following advantages."

There follow in the Draft six "advantages", of which three
are embodied in section 22 as published. Nos. 1, 5 and 6 of the
Draft appear now as Nos. 1, 2 and 3. Nos. 2, 3 and 4 have
disappeared; No. 2 claimed to have abridged the trouble of
examining notions; No. 3 claimed that fewer objects to consider

* *Works*, Vol. II, p. 247.
† See *Works*, Vol. II, pp. 141–2.

were left, and No. 4 claimed a clearer prospect of the ideas that remain. These omissions do not amount to very much; but they have interest as showing the importance Berkeley attached to his notebooks, and the use he made of them in revising and drafting. No less than three entries, now lost to view, No. 642 on "the mist or veil of words", No. 600 on "emptiness & scarcity of ideas", and No. 737 on "the deformity of Errour" appear on one page of the Draft.

The conceit of the Solitary Man is rather far-fetched, and Berkeley was right to omit it. From his misconceived attempt to think without speaking Berkeley learned much; he learned to value words; and few philosophers have equalled him in his sense of the power of words and in the art of using the proper word in the proper place and the proper order. Perhaps the following entry voiced for him the conclusion of the whole matter:

✗   *Words (by them meaning all sort of signs) are so neces-sary that instead of being (wn duly us'd or in their own Nature) prejudicial to the Advancement of knowlege, or an hindrance to knowlege that wthout them there could in Mathematiques themselves be no demonstration.*

(No. 750)

CHAPTER VIII

THE EXPANSION OF THE PRINCIPLE

OF unthinking things, Berkeley says* "their *esse* is *percipi*", taking up and applying his statement in the *Commentaries* (No. 429). "Existence is percipi . . ." *Esse est percipi.* By its Latin title Berkeley's Principle has passed into history; but that title is an abbreviation; it covers part of the Principle only; and if that part is taken for the whole, the Principle itself is compromised, and grave injustice is done to Berkeley's philosophy.

Berkeley's first concern was with the actually perceived; he could not say everything all at once; but he took things in order due, and he set himself to determine the status and nature of what we actually perceive when we are perceiving it. It exists, he says; it is; and its being or existence is *to be perceived*; for that is what the terms *being* and *existence* mean. We smell a smell and take in its existence with the sniff. We see a book and see that it is. In touching a table we touch an existing table. We taste strawberries, and can no more doubt their existence than we can doubt our own. We hear the sound of the horn and the cry of the hounds and then the View Halloo; and these sounds self-evidently exist; they are perceived. These are intuitive truths; one sees them *par simple vue*. On the other hand to add "and it exists" to "I see the table" is a gratuitous, misleading addition to a complete self-explanatory statement. The table could not be seen, if it did not exist; the notion of an invisible, intangible, insensible table *existing* is a contradiction, like a hot snowball or a round square. *Esse est percipi*; there is more to be said, and there are inferences to be drawn; the Principle must expand and grow; but there it is in its germinal state. To be is to be perceived. That was Berkeley's discovery, the secret of his

* *Principles*, section 3.

intellectual conversion, the controlling motive and mainspring of the revision of 1707–8.

The first effect of the discovery was retrospective. Looking back Berkeley saw in it a confirmation of the immaterial hypothesis on which he had been working for some three years past; he regarded it as a conclusive disproof of the existence of material substance. The Principle was a new weapon of high calibre. Being intuitive it was independent of the laborious and inconclusive argumentation by which Malebranche and Bayle had built up their case against matter. Following out their line Berkeley in his first arguings had argued that the qualities of things are in the mind and therefore not in matter. Now he can dispense with that line, and go straight to the point, viz. the nature of existence and the meaning of the term *exist*. Matter cannot be perceived; therefore (if the Principle is sound) matter cannot exist. That was the first major effect of the discovery of the Principle; it saved the immaterial hypothesis, and salvaged much of the work of Berkeley's Fellowship thesis. At the same time it contributed positively to the revision itself. Freed from his previous dependence on Malebranche and mentalism, he re-found his native common sense, rejected panpsychism and learned anew to trust his senses, and to trust them intelligently. These changes worked like leaven. Sensible body, perceived and perceivable, mind, spirit, will and understanding could now be freely discussed, and as the revision progressed week by week and month by month, the full doctrine of the *Principles* grew to maturity and found expression.

Esse est percipi. It is a complete statement about the existence of the object of actual perception; it is not a complete statement about existence. Berkeley's first concern was the object of actual perception; but he could not ignore the other types of existent; sooner or later he had to make up his mind about the subject perceiving and about the possible object of perception. In due course the nature of their existence must be discussed and determined. The Principle must expand to take them in; otherwise it would be lopsided and incomplete. There must therefore be two major extensions of the formula. They are implicit in the perceptual situation as Berkeley saw it; and they were recognized, and in part named by him. They are (a) the existence of the subject perceiving, and (b) the existence of the potential object of perception. Neither of them falls under the formula as it was originally worded by Berkeley and as it is usually worded by philosophers; but they both fall under the Principle, and its formula expands naturally to take them in, as the following *recto–verso* entry shows:

E   *Existence is percipi or percipere/. the horse is in the stable,
       the Books are in the study as before.*

                                                    (No. 429)
                  (on the facing page)
                  /or velle i :e. agere
                                                    (No. 429a)

It is an intriguing pair of entries, illustrating both the expansion of the Principle (on the *recto*) and the later rise of the will to psychological pre-eminence (on the *verso*). Note the marginal letter "E". Berkeley is consciously addressing himself to the nature and meaning and import of *existence*, and he is breaking new ground. He has already dealt with passive existence, the existence of unthinking things, the inanimate side of reality; here for the first time he points his pen at active existence, and writes on the existence of thinking things, on the existence of spirits, yours and mine, on the animate side of reality.

If something is perceived, there must be a perceiver. If changes are willed, there must be someone that wills. If actions are done, they are done by an agent. The perceiver exists; the will exists; the agent exists. But what *is* their existence? It is not *percipi*; that is not what we mean when we assert the existence of percipient, willing, active beings. What then do we mean? Berkeley answers that the existence of the percipient is *percipere*, and that when we say the percipient *exists*, we mean that he perceives. It is hard to see what else it could mean. To say "I perceive the table, and I exist" would be just as ridiculous as to say, "I perceive the table and it exists." I could not perceive the table unless I existed, and by and in perceiving I *pro tanto* exist and am. *Percipio, ergo sum.*

Accordingly Berkeley makes the first addition to his formula. *Esse est percipere*; and if *percipere* is used in its broad sense to cover all the activities of the mind of man, then *esse est percipi aut percipere* would be an expansion of the Principle adequate to cover the existence of both factors in the actual perceptual situation. But as Berkeley developed his philosophy of the mind and spirit, the will was elevated to the primacy, and understanding and perception took second place; and he added on the facing page "or velle i:e. agere". It matters little whether the first addition to the formula be 'percipere' or 'velle' or 'agere', provided the addition be made; but the addition is vital to a sane interpretation of Berkeley's philosophy. The *esse est percipi* remained for Berkeley the focus of interest, and remains so for us; the *object* of perception is the more important thing when immaterialism is discussed; but a constructive philosophy of immaterialism cannot be built on the *esse est percipi* alone. *Esse est percipi* is a far-reaching statement about the object perceived, but it is a dangerous statement unless accompanied and balanced by a complementary statement about the subject perceiving. If *esse est percipi* be true, as Berkeley held, it is certainly not the whole truth. If it were the whole truth, then your *esse*, reader, and mine would be *percipi*; you and I would be only what in us is seen and touched and otherwise perceived by sense; the same would hold of the existence of God; all existence would be passive; spirits would be as inactive as stocks and stones; in other words they would not be spirits at all. The perceptual situation would melt away, and be reduced to a name and a shadow. A perceived implies a perceiver, and a perceiver implies a perceived; *percipi* and *percipere* imply the one the other, and until *percipere* is expressly included in it, the formula for Berkeley's discovery remains incomplete. The two sides of the Principle are clearly recognized in the following entry:

S   *Things are two-fold active or inactive. The Existence of Active things is to act, of inactive to be perceiv'd.*

(No. 673)

The *esse est percipi* will always attract the more attention; but the *esse est percipere* is of equal importance; for the two terms *percipere* and *percipi* represent "the two kinds entirely distinct and heterogeneous . . . spirits and ideas"* which are the twin pillars of Berkeley's philosophy. Without the active being, infinite and finite, that is, without the mind and will of God and man, Berkeley's philosophy would drop to pieces. There must be Infinite spirit to give ideas, and a finite spirit to receive ideas, and the ideas must be from and for the spirit. Without the passive being, that is, without the idea-things that constitute sensible reality and the world of sense, Berkeley's published philosophy would drop to the level of his first arguings, according to which only conscious things exist.

If we may pause to take a wider canvas and look beyond Berkeley to the history of philosophy itself, two instances stand out in which confusion has been caused by taking *existence* as a simple uniform concept the same in all that is. In his fifth Meditation Descartes says he is accustomed to distinguish between existence and essence, and that existence can be separated from the essence of God, until he thinks of the case more attentively, and then he finds that existence can no more be separated from the essence of God than the equality of its angles to two right angles can be separated from the essence of a triangle. It is a confusing passage, and the confusion rests largely on the comparison, drawn by Descartes, between an essentially active Being and an essentially passive thing. If that be true of a concept like a triangle, it is even more clearly true of a percept like one hundred dollars in my pocket. The dollars exist. I see and feel them; their *esse* is *percipi*; their essence is passive. They were placed in my pocket and they stayed there till they were taken out. Philosophers ignore that distinction

* *Principles*, section 89.

who argue that the *Ens realissimum* must exist because, containing all reality, it must contain in its concept the notion of existence. In that argument, too, existence is treated as a single notion, than can be attached and detached, put away in a box or hung like a garland round the neck. And Kant equally with those whom he refutes in this matter falls into the existence-trap. He fails to notice, or conveniently ignores, that existence relates to the existent; and he speaks of the passive existence of the dollars as if it were comparable with the active existence of the universal Spirit in whom we live and move and are.

Esse est percipi aut percipere. It is a rich and fruitful predication about things of sense and God and man. *Esse est percipi*; then I can trust my senses; the sensible objects I perceive are *pro tanto* completely known; they are not a mysterious unknowable, something we know not what; they are not matter, nor haunted by matter. *Esse est percipere*; then the divine existence is no dubious concept or passive attribute, but ceaseless activity of boundless will and thought. *Esse est percipere*; then the existence of finite spirits is not a bare abstract continuance, but a concrete process and progress. *Esse est percipere*; then human existence is a movement, an evolution, a task and enterprise, and it may be a growth in intellectual and moral stature, in learning, knowledge, wisdom and the other values of the spirit.

Potentiality is the other crux. The Principle must expand further; it must be elastic enough to cover possible existence. Berkeley had to come to terms with mind when it is not minding, and with the perceivable when we are not perceiving it. He had difficulties with both parts of the problem and he changed his mind about it more than once. His readers find it a perplexing point. "The objects of sense exist only when they are perceived; the trees therefore are in the garden, or the chairs in the parlour, no longer than while there is some body by to perceive them. Upon shutting my eyes all the furniture in the room is reduced to nothing, and barely upon opening them it is again created."* Are those Berkeley's own opinions, or those of

* *Principles*, section 45. See above, p. 34.

his antagonist? Readers of that passage are often in doubt, and Berkeley is in no hurry to enlighten us. To keep us in doubt was part of his method. He was long in doubt himself.

Let us watch him wrestling with the problem in his note-book: we must repeat the entry with the accent this time on the second half:

E   *Existence is percipi or percipere. the horse is in the stable, the Books are in the study as before.*

(No. 429)

It is a curious *non-sequitur* at first sight; but the context explains it. The horse in the stable and the books in the study are Berkeley's working examples of perceivables unperceived. "We see the horse itself," he has just said (No. 427). There it is in the paddock. We see *it*. *It* is an idea, an immediate object, "& nothing more". There is no "second" or "other" horse. There is no material or absolute or original horse. There is no horse over and above the horse we see or ride or back. Paddy puts the horse in the stable and locks the door. I return to the house and my reading and forget the horse. The horse is now unperceived; does he cease to be? "No," says Berkeley, "the horse is in the stable . . . as before." And what about the books when they are unperceived? Now I see them; there they are on the study table, a folio copy of Locke's *Essay* and Malebranche's *Recherche* in quarto. I leave them there and go out for a walk. I meet you. "You ask me whether the books are in the study now wn no one is there to see them." (No. 472.) Yes, the books are in the study, as before.

Berkeley when he penned that entry had still a long way to go before he reached the full doctrine of the *Principles* on the point. He had still to deal explicitly with the reality of body (see below, pp. 133 ff.); he had still to ask and answer the questions, In what sense are horse and books in stable and study, respect-ively, when there is nobody by to perceive them? And how can their existence then be reconciled with the Principle? But he has taken a decisive step; he has asserted their existence, and *eo ipso* he has parted with his panpsychist past. A man of his strong common sense, a man shortly to be charged with the College discipline of politically minded Irish students on the eve of an *emeute*, such a man could have no patience with vanishing horses, disappearing books and intermittent Cheshire cats. In some sense, Berkeley realized, the things we see and touch must continue to exist over the gaps in actual perception. In a tenable immaterialism possible perception must have its proper place, side by side with actual perception; and once committed to the Principle, *esse est percipi*, he was bound to follow it up with *esse est posse percipi*. Berkeley does not make that addition to his formula in terms, but he does so by implication in the entry quoted above (No. 429), where after adding *percipere* explicitly to the formula he at once goes on to assert the existence unperceived of the horse in the stable and the books in the study.

Other entries clinch this conclusion. As we all do in ordinary life, Berkeley freely uses terms of possibility and terms of actuality interchangeably, as if they had identical status. In No. 28, for instance, motion, figure and extension "perceivable by sight" stand side by side with "those ideas perceived by touch". In Nos. 35, 249 and 250 the term "perceivable" is used without any suggestion of non-actuality; "perceived" could be substituted without affecting the sense. The term "edible mushroom", for instance, applies no less to a mushroom that has been eaten than to one that has not been eaten. A striking example of this interchange occurs when Berkeley is studying the composition of geometrical figures. He expressly identifies what is there with what you may see, but are not actually seeing; he accepts possible existence as possible perception. He writes:

✗   *Mem: nicely to discuss wt is meant when we say a line consists of a certain number of inches or points etc A Circle of a certain number of square inches, points etc. Certainly we may think of a Circle, or have its' idea in*

> *our mind without thinking of points or square inches etc.*
> *whence it should seem the idea of a Circle is not made up*
> *of the ideas of points square inches etc.*
>
> (No. 445)

✗   *Qu: is any more than this meant by the foregoing*
> *Expressions viz. that squares or points may be perceived*
> *in or made out of a Circle etc. or that squares points etc.*
> *are actually in it i.e. are perceivable in it.*
>
> (No. 446)

In the concluding words beyond all doubt Berkeley attributes
actual existence to squares and points that may be perceived in
a circle, and explains that actual existence as possible perception. Here then is a confessed expansion of the Principle, and
the *posse percipi* takes its place beside the *percipi*. This line of
thought accepts possible existence as possible perception, and
it comes to full fruition towards the end of notebook A in the
important entry:

M.P   *Not to mention the Combinations of Powers but to say the*
> *things the effects themselves to really exist even wn not*
> *actually perceiv'd but still with relation to perception.*
>
> (No. 802)

This is a very broad statement about the things that constitute
the external world; they have real existence even when not
actually perceived; but their existence is not material or
absolute; it is sensible and relative, always in relation to perception, perceivable, when not actually perceived.

The result of Berkeley's long debate on body and the
perceivable is thus quite clear; there are real bodies and they
exist even when they are not actually perceived by us; but they
have not the existence commonly attributed to matter; for
matter *ex hypothesi* is imperceptible and unrelated to perception;
whereas the real things around us are always in relation to
perception, and can always be perceived by sense. The status of
unperceived existence is thus clarified and secured, and this

great step forward was made possible by the elasticity of the Principle that controlled the whole revision and the development of Berkeley's thought. The Principle must expand and did expand; otherwise Berkeley would have been left with that narrow interpretation of the *esse est percipi* that consigns to nothingness all that man is not actually perceiving.

Berkeley makes this development himself on his first mention of the Principle in his published work; for as soon as he has applied the Principle to the table actually perceived, he proceeds to extend it to the table he did not perceive, adding

"and if I were out of my study I should say it [my table] existed, meaning thereby that if I was in my study I might perceive it, or that some other spirit actually does perceive it."*

Thus in his books and in his notebooks Berkeley is committed to the common-sense view of unperceived existence, and when we take account of all the facets of his problem, viz. actual and possible perception, the subject perceiving and the object perceived, Berkeley's Principle *esse est percipi* expands with his approval and consent into the formula, *Esse est percipi aut posse percipi, aut percipere aut posse percipere.*

It remains to sketch the application of the expanded Principle to the revision of 1707–8. The Principle determined the lines of that revision. The discoverer's joy evidenced first in notebook B in entries 265, 266, 270 and 279, and later in notebook A in Nos. 410, 430, 556 and 682, is also the reviser's joy at the prospect of a fruitful revision with the assurance that past work was not labour lost. The young author is now a happy man, he has discovered something in philosophy; he has found his north-west passage; he can set course for immaterialism without fear of the rocks of materialism or the quicksands of scepticism. He has discovered, he thinks, an axiomatic disproof of material substance, and the clumsy, inconclusive weapon on which he relied formerly can now be scrapped. No longer does

* *Principles*, section 3.

I

he need Malebranche and Bayle; no longer does he lean on their writings; no longer is he tied to their arguments. No longer does his case rest on the subjectivity of primary and secondary qualities. It now rests on the nature and meaning and import of *existence*.

To be is to be perceived; material substance cannot be perceived, and cannot be. To be is to be perceived; perceived things are, and are what they are perceived to be. To be is to be perceived; there are things perceiving as well as things perceived. To be is to perceive; there are perceivers and they do perceive. Finally, to be is to be able to perceive, and to be able to be perceived. Thus materialism and mentalism cancel out, and on the vacant site Berkeley builds his revised philosophy of spirit and sense without matter.

CHAPTER IX

BODY

In this critical chapter we reach the crux of Berkeleian interpretation and the heart of the revision. Did Berkeley believe in
the real existence of body, and teach it? That is the crux. He
left instructions in his Will about the disposal of his own body
after death. He spent time and thought on experiments with tar
and acids and salts in an attempt to cure the ills of the body. Is
his published philosophy consistent with the beliefs implied by
those actions? He denied the existence of matter; did he *eo ipso*
deny the existence of body? Or did he so deny the existence of
matter as to affirm *eo ipso* the existence of body? A first answer
to these queries is given by the following important entry,
already quoted:

M   *On second thoughts I am, on t'other extream I am certain
       of that wch Malbranch seems to doubt of. viz the exist-
       ence of Bodies.*

(No. 686a)

Berkeley wrote those words without any thought of anyone
else reading them, and they can mean only one thing, viz. that
he had previously doubted, if not denied, the existence of body,
had gone from the one extreme to the other, and was now
certain of the existence of body. It was an extraordinary right-
about-face; but we can see the reasons for it, and can follow it
intelligently stage by stage by studying the relevant entries in
the notebooks.

There are over forty entries dealing with body. Berkeley went
thoroughly into the question, and as we follow the windings of
his path, we shall see the gradual replacement of his first
thoughts by his second.

Berkeley's first thoughts on body came to him with the

immaterial hypothesis from Malebranche, who in the *excursus*, outlined above (p. 65), shows the difficulty of *proving* the existence of body, and rests the case for it, not on reason, but on the Christian faith. By reason, he says, we only know the existence of God and our own souls, and apart from our faith, the appearance of bodies would serve the purposes of life just as well as their real existence. That was Berkeley's position when he began his revision, and looking back on it some twelve months later, he wrote:

M.P.E.   *Malbranch in his Illustration differs widely from me He doubts of the existence of Bodies I doubt not in the least of this.*

(No. 800)

P   *I differ from the Cartesians in that I make extension, Colour etc to exist really in Bodies & independent of Our Mind. All ys carefully & lucidly to be set forth.*

(No. 801)

"I doubt not in the least of this." Much hard thinking had to be done before Berkeley could pen those confident words. Two thousand years or so of uncriticized belief in material substance lay behind him, and it was not easy for him to see how to reconcile immaterialism with the real existence of a world of bodies, independent of our minds. Nor is *our* task easy. There is no intrinsic difficulty in Berkeley's view of the external world. Great thinkers, great artists, great men of action lived before Aristotle invented matter and coined a word for it. It is not the facts of life, but the history of thought that makes immaterialism hard to expound and understand. The scales are weighted against Berkeley. That is why the following study is so instructive. We shall see the reasons why he first doubted and denied the existence of body, and then came round to believe in it. We shall see him at the danger-points; we shall see him on the slippery slope, recovering his balance, and feeling his way back to sanity and common sense. We shall see him doubting, and frightened of his doubts, as the spectre of scepticism looms large and near. We shall see him experimenting in compromise and half-measures, and then rejecting them. Finally we shall see him, as he reaches the end of notebook A, satisfied that a world of sensible bodies exists, independent of our minds, but adapted to them, and grounded in the universal Mind.

I sketched above (p. 27) in free style the movement of Berkeley's thought on the question of body. I must now fill in the details of the sketch, and substantiate my argument. First, consider together two entries from near the beginning of the *Commentaries*, and one from towards the end:

+   *Nothing corresponds to our primary ideas wthout but powers, hence a direct & brief demonstration of an active powerfull being distinct from us on whom we depend. etc.*

                                                  (No. 41)

+   *Bodies etc do exist even wn not perceiv'd they being powers in the active Being.*

                                                  (No. 52)

M.P   *Not to mention the Combinations of Powers but to say the things the effects themselves to really exist even wn not actually perceiv'd but still with relation to perception.*
                                                 (No. 802)

The pendulum has swung far. In the two early entries, both obelized, both discarded, bodies are virtually explained away. In the late, third entry the *powers* theory is shelved, and the existence of bodies is affirmed as definitely as any realist could desire. The *things*, the effects themselves, really exist, and the combinations of powers are not to be mentioned.

Berkeley's *powers* theory of body was a spiritualized form of Locke's theory. Locke taught that the secondary qualities "are but the powers of several combinations of those primary ones, when they operate without being distinctly discerned",* and

* *Essay*, II, viii, 22.

he gave point to his teaching by the following passage on memory and the percept; "if I turn my eyes at noon towards the sun, I cannot avoid the ideas which the light or sun then produces in me." Locke infers "the brisk acting of some objects without me, whose efficacy I cannot resist".* In section 29 of the *Principles* Berkeley uses the same illustration, but transforms and spiritualizes it by substituting "some other will or spirit" for Locke's "light or sun"; and he was making the parallel transformation when he substituted combinations of powers in God for Locke's combinations of powers in the primary qualities of matter.

Berkeley never varied in his belief that there are powers in God; but that is not the point here. The point is that when he penned that entry at the start of the revision, he held and taught that the combinations of powers in God *are* (what we call) bodies. At that time he did not recognize anything else "without us", and "bodies" had to be powers in God, or nothing. I see the top surface of the table on which I write; it is a visual idea in my mind. I could see its other surfaces, which are not now in my mind; and we call the table a *body*. By what right? By the same right that Shakespeare has to call Macbeth's dagger in the mind a *body*. He calls it into bodily form when he wishes, gives me to see it, and sets its handle next my twitching fingers. My table exists as a combination of powers in God, as Macbeth's dagger exists as a combination of powers in Shakespeare. It is an ingenious paper theory, but obviously a *tour de force*. It meets some difficulties in the immaterial hypothesis, but gives rise to greater difficulties.

The *powers* theory of body was the linch-pin of Berkeley's unrevised immaterialism. He was forced into it by the exigencies of his panpsychist outlook. He knew that he must assert the existence of body, or be branded as a sceptic and be a sceptic, and throughout the summer and autumn of 1707 he asserted it in a sense that takes all reality out of it. In the earlier part of notebook B Berkeley asserts that bodies *are* powers in

* ib. IV, xi, 5.

God. Being a panpsychist then he could not make body the *effect* of God's powers; to do so would be the same as saying that God makes us see and touch bodies that are not there. No. Berkeley did not make God a deceiver; he did not then say that bodies were the effects of divine powers; he said they *were* the divine powers. That position is untenable; it is inconsistent with theism, and is little short of pantheism; it does not translate into any theory of actual sense-perception. Its only interest today is that Berkeley at first held it, and then gave it up.

Compromise on the existence of body dominates notebook B. Berkeley will spiritualize body; he will concede it an unreal or nominal existence; but all through this period he clung tenaciously to his bodiless world of mind and conscious things; and then when autumn passed into winter, overborne by the fear of scepticism, he began to consider an alternative; he gave serious thought to sense without matter. Helped by the discovery of the Principle, he began to conceive a non-mental world of real, sensible bodies, immaterial, stable and independent of our minds, perceivable, when not actually perceived. When he opened his second notebook in the winter of 1707–8, he began it with a full sense of the existence of real body, though some minor difficulties remained to be cleared up.

From this broad survey of the period of doubt I turn to chapter and verse. The entries dealing with body in notebook B are Nos. 41, 52, 79–80, 84, 98 (on *verso*), 185, 185a, 228, 282, 288, 293, 293a, 298, 304, 305, 312, 339 and 391. Note that Nos. 282–312 (the largest group) come in a bunch very soon after the discovery of the Principle. That discovery altered the situation about body. The Principle, carefully considered, permits and postulates the existence of real body, perceived and perceivable; and in finding the meaning of the term *exist* when applied to sensible things, Berkeley learned how to reconcile the existence of body with the immaterial hypothesis.

I have already commented on Nos. 41 and 52, and need only add a remark on the queer phrase "Bodies etc" which occurs in the latter. The "etc" may have no significance at all;* if it means anything here, it must refer to the constituents of body, such as qualities, ideas or sensations, or to bodies under another name, such as *things* or *substances*.

Two entries follow that show Berkeley at a halfway house:

M   *Mem. that I take notice that I do not fall in with Sceptics Fardella etc in yt I make bodies to exist certainly* ('*wthout us*', prima manu) *wch they doubt of.*

(No. 79)

M   *I am more certain of ye existence & reality of Bodies than Mr. Locke since he pretends onely to wt he calls sensitive knowlege, whereas I think I have demonstrative knowlege of their Existence, by them meaning combinations of powers in an unknown substratum.*

(No. 80)

Berkeley had read in Bayle (see above, p. 69) of the Sicilian monk, Fardella, whose case was so like his own. See what comes, he said to himself, of doubting the existence of body.

The manuscript shows a small but significant correction. At first Berkeley wrote, "I make bodies to exist wthout us." Then he had a qualm; did he really believe in bodies "without us"? No, he did not; only a page or two back he had written that there is nothing outside but God and powers in God. He took his pen, struck out the offending words, and substituted *certainly*. In the following entry he explains his "certainly". He is more certain than Locke, who claimed only *sensitive* knowledge† of the real existence of bodies, whereas he (Berkeley) thinks he has demonstrative knowledge of them, meaning by *them* "combinations of powers in an unknown substratum".

It is a profession of relative certainty, and is far from con-

---

* Berkeley was very free with his "etceteras" in his notebooks and, indeed, in the first edition of the *Principles*; forty-one etceteras were removed in the second edition.

† *Essay*, IV, ii, 14.

vincing. Berkeley was dodging the issue, or he was self-deceived.
He may have been more certain than Locke, and later (Nos.
547, 563) he claimed intuitive knowledge of the existence of
external things. At the earlier stage the assertion was made for
tactical purposes, and only covered the existence of shadowy
powers in an unknown substratum.

Berkeley remained at this halfway house for some weeks, and
the next entry on the subject finds him still there. This entry is
doubly instructive if read along with Berkeley's comment on the
facing page, and I print the two as they stand in the manuscript:

	(verso)		(recto)
M.P	*Colours in ye dark do exist really i.e were there light or as soon as light comes we shall see them provided we open our eyes. & that whether we will or no.*	M.P.	*Mem: to allow existence to colours in the dark, persons not thinking &c but not an absolute actual existence. 'Tis prudent to correct mens mistakes without altering their language. This makes truth glide into their souls insensibly.*
	(No. 185a)		(No. 185)

The *recto* entry, obviously written before the *verso*, attempts to
justify a tactical refinement about the unperceived perceivable
("colours in the dark") and the unperceiving percipient
("persons not thinking"). He will concede them a nominal
existence, not an absolute actual existence. That can only
mean that he will keep intermittency to himself until he has
accustomed his readers to the new climate of thought; he hopes
thus to alter his readers' views without altering their language
and to let truth glide insensibly into their souls. Berkeley still
held the *powers* theory; for him then there was no red rose other
than the combination of powers in God to dispose us to see the

rose and its colours when light comes and we look. He still held the intermittent existence of the human mind or soul.

The *verso* entry (No. 185a) is in strong contrast. It does not mention tactical refinements, or hint at a deliberate economy of truth; it does not mention the intermittency of the subject, and it explicitly asserts the real, relative existence of colours in the dark, subject of course to the conditions of vision—light and open eyes; the colours are there to see, and we shall see them in daytime, if we do our part. There is no mention of the *powers* theory; the colours are not identified with God's disposition to make us see them, or with our disposition to see them. For these reasons the verso cannot be regarded as an explanation, written at the time; it is a correction of the *recto*, written months afterwards. If No. 185a were simply an explanation of No. 185, the two entries would have been in sequence on the *recto*. In point of fact No. 185a on the face of it *is* a correction, and goes far beyond an explanation; it is part and parcel of Berkeley's second thoughts on body, and should be read along with Nos. 800–2, where Berkeley records his final opinion about body, as published in the *Principles*. When Berkeley wrote the *recto* entry (No. 185) he was still at his halfway house, not believing in the existence of body, but casting about for some account of appearances that would look as if he did. When he wrote the *verso* comment (No. 185a), he had taken the great decision. No more putative existence, no more quibbles about real and dispositional existence—when he wrote that colours in the dark exist really, he was using words in their natural meaning.

Midway through notebook B, Berkeley showed precisely where he stood in the following summary statement:

M   *All things by us conceivable are 1st thoughts 2dly powers to receive thoughts, 3dly powers to cause thoughts neither of all wch can possibly exist in an inert, senseless thing.*

(No. 228)

"Thoughts" include sensible things, considered as modes of consciousness; "powers to receive thoughts" are the percipient powers of the human mind; "powers to cause thoughts" are the powers of the infinite spirit and the powers of the human mind to frame images. When he made this note, Berkeley's universe consisted of God, human minds and their thoughts; but he was moving towards a change; for he winds up the entry by declaring that none of these things can exist in matter; he is on the point of discovering his Principle.

Berkeley then turned to other topics, and when next he deals with body he has discovered his Principle and has begun to reconstruct his philosophy.

The following entries break new ground:

+   *Bodies etc do ['really', erased] exist whether we think of 'em or no, they being taken in a twofold sense. Collections of thoughts & collections of powers to cause those thoughts. these later exist, tho perhaps a parte dei it may be one simple perfect power.*

(No. 282)

+   *The twofold signification of Bodies viz. combinations of thoughts & combinations of powers to raise thoughts. These, I say, in conjunction with homogeneous particles, may solve much better the objections from the Creation. than ye supposition that matter does exist upon wch supposition, I think, they cannot be solvd.*

(No. 293)

+   *Bodies taken for Powers do exist wn not perceiv'd but this existence is not actual. wn I say a power exists no more is meant than that if in ye light I open my eyes & look that way I shall see it i.e. yt body &c.*

(No. 293a)

Here Berkeley accepts for the time being *two* meanings of the term *body*, viz. collections of thoughts and collections of powers to cause them. It was a further attempt at compromise. Berkeley was driven to it, I believe, by the pressure of his

Creation problem, which probably brought to a head the issue about body. The compromise on the face of it is bad; the one term could not have two meanings so diametrically opposed. Berkeley's system in particular could not admit active body and passive body; and, for him, if the effects are bodies, then the causes of those effects cannot also be bodies, as No. 293a virtually admits. All three entries are obelized, and we hear no more of "the twofold signification of Bodies". Temporarily, however, the distinction was of great importance; it was the beginning of the end of the *powers* theory. Body as a collection of powers in God was to disappear, and body as a collection of thoughts was to remain, and become *the collection of ideas* of section 1 of the *Principles*.

We must now look carefully at "the objections from the Creation" of No. 293; for the attempt to compromise about body involved an attempt to compromise about the creation of body. For a time Berkeley had it in mind to argue that in one sense of that term God created body, and in another sense He created only the appearance of body, and a disposition in us to perceive body. These two meanings, he says, would solve the problems, in conjunction with homogeneous particles, much better than the supposition of matter. There is much to be explained here.

First, what are "the objections from the Creation"? They are, (a) the general difficulties which beset all thought about origins, especially the coming of something out of nothing, (b) Berkeley's special difficulties, the creation of body other than mind, and the Mosaic order which places the creation of man after that of other things. In the *Commentaries* Berkeley refers to general questions about creation in Nos. 339, 830 and 831, and to his special difficulties about it in Nos. 60, 293, 436 and 723. He will bring in homogeneous particles to meet the objection of the sun and plants etc. being created before animals (No. 60). In the entry under discussion (No. 293) he hopes to solve that problem by aid of the particles in conjunction with the twofold meaning of bodies. Bodies were

created before man, just as light was created before man
(No. 436). There were other intelligences before man, and
therefore he can say that earth and plants etc. were created
before man (No. 723). In the *Three Dialogues** Berkeley discusses Creation at length, gives his own account and answers
the specific objections brought against his system. In his letter
to Percival of 6 September 1710† he answers Lady Percival's
pointed query, viz. If God created only spirits and ideas, what
do you make of the things He created before He created man?
He does not deal with this specific difficulty in the *Principles*,
and, but for the notebooks, we should not have known of the
careful thought he had given to the difficulty five years before
he published the *Dialogues*.

The supposition of matter is no solution of the difficulties
about the Creation, Berkeley says; and he is obviously right
there. Apart altogether from the historical facts that the Jews,
like the Greeks before Aristotle, had no word for matter, and
that there is not the slightest hint of the creation of matter in
the Mosaic story of creation or anywhere in the Bible,‡ the
supposition of the creation of a material sun, for instance,
leaves untouched the question of the visible and tangible sun
which (Moses says) was created before Adam.

Setting matter aside Berkeley finds help in two distinct lines
of thought, and hopes to solve his problem by their aid, viz. the
double meaning of the term *body* and homogeneous particles.
The latter had been in his mind for some time; he spoke of
them in Nos. 60 and 64; the former had only just then come to
him, one would think; it was only a passing thought, and the
fact that he gave it attention and devoted three entries to it is
proof of the intellectual straits to which he was reduced by the

---

* *Works*, Vol. II, pp. 250 ff.

† *Works*, Vol. VIII, p. 37.

‡ Matter entered Christian theology through the non-canonical books,
known as the Apocrypha, especially the *Book of Wisdom*. These books,
written under Aristotelian influence, were accepted by the Greek-speaking
Jews of Alexandria, but not by the Palestinians.

Creation difficulty. Lady Percival felt it a serious difficulty in Berkeley's system; any thoughtful person at that time would feel it so; and Berkeley had no answer, nor way of escape, as long as he clung to his bodiless world of mind.

Before he thought of this "twofold signification" Berkeley's Creation problem was insoluble. While he viewed bodies only as powers in God, he could not consistently accept anything as created before man, and the very notion of creation was imperilled. If God created only human minds and modes of mind, the works of the first five Days of creation would be null and void. Even Omnipotence could not create Adam on Friday, and Adam's thoughts, dispositions, perceptions and feelings on the previous Thursday. Berkeley was in a cleft stick. He had to choose between Moses and his own first arguings, between real body and nebulous powers in God. That is why the Creation problem was a turning-point in the development of his thought about body. But now the panpsychist phase was passing. Berkeley was beginning to see bodies in a new light; they are no longer for him only powers in deity; as well they are thought-things, combinations of things-for-thought, and there is no reason at all why *such* objects should not be created before man, and every reason why they should. The evolutionist postulates the environment as prior to the evolving organism; and the creation of light and heat and the other requirements of life before man fits logically into Berkeley's scheme of creative evolution. Berkeley says that it is consistent with his principles to conceive Creation as the production by an invisible power of "a parcel of plants or vegetables of all sorts . . . in a desert where no body was present."* He says it is consistent with his principles; he does not say it is the most intelligent way of conceiving creation. It is consistent with his principles, because the plants and vegetables after their kinds are there, really there, though nobody is there to see or eat them. They were created; *ergo sunt*. At the time of making the entry Berkeley called them *collections of thoughts*; in his *Principles* he called

* *Works*, Vol. II, p. 252.

them *collections of ideas*; but once he had fairly and squarely faced his difficulties about the Creation, and *ex animo* accepted a real creation, he could no longer call the plants and vegetables *collections of powers in God.*

Here is the nerve-centre of the passage in the *Dialogues*:*

HYLAS. The Scripture account of the Creation, is what appears to me utterly irreconcileable with your notions. Moses tells us of a Creation: a Creation of what? of ideas? No certainly, but of things, of real things, solid corporeal substances. Bring your principles to agree with this, and I shall perhaps agree with you.

PHILONOUS. Moses mentions the sun, moon, and stars, earth and sea, plants and animals: that all these do really exist, and were in the beginning created by God, I make no question. . . . I imagine that if I had been present at the Creation, I should have seen things produced into being; that is, become perceptible, in the order described by the sacred historian. I ever before believed the Mosaic account of the Creation, and now find no alteration in my manner of believing it.

Berkeley did not, however, believe *unintelligently* in creation. Longinus called the *fiat lux* sublime; and Berkeley would have no "Hey Presto" magic in his thought of origins. "With a leap and a bound the flexible tiger appears." We accept such events in religious poetry, but not in sober philosophy. In his thoughts on creation Berkeley ever had an eye to the rationality of our minds and the rationality of the universe, and in conceiving it, with Moses, as the gradual evolution of a historical drama in six Days or Ages, he gave serious thought to the possibility, or indeed the probability, of the existence of created intelligent spirits other than man. Berkeley speaks in the *Dialogues* on the point with natural reserve as we today speak of life and thought in other planets. He virtually says that it is not for him to prove the affirmative, but for Hylas and his followers to prove the

* *Works*, Vol. II, pp. 250-1.

negative. He had long had the point in mind (see No. 723). It was a speculative point for him, as it is for us; and he leaves us at liberty to conceive his parcel of plants and vegetables in an unpeopled world, awaiting the coming of man, if we prefer to do so. But he nowhere asks us to believe that there would have been no grass for the cattle in the pre-Adamite world, unless the angels had been there to pasture them.

A further proof of Berkeley's attempt to reach a rational notion of creative evolution is his brief reference in our entry to "homogeneous particles". He says that the two meanings of *body*, taken in conjunction with homogeneous particles, may solve his Creation difficulties. This can only mean that the collections of thoughts, forming the one aspect of body, *are* the homogeneous particles. Berkeley has published no statement about them, I think; but from his notebooks we can gather what was in his mind.

To begin with, the term *homogeneous* must be specialized and technical. Particles, homogeneous with one another, would be presumably atoms, which would not be helpful to Berkeley in any connection. There can be little doubt that the particles in view are homogeneous with the wholes of which they are part, and that they represent the *homoiomeries* of Anaxagoras, or some adaptation of them. Berkeley would have met the homo-iomeries in the history of philosophy and in Bacon;* but he probably owed his special interest in them to Bayle's article *Anaxagoras*. Bayle calls them *homogeneities*, and says that Anaxa-goras made use of them in order to avoid having to admit a creation *de nihilo*. The special reason for linking them with Berkeley's homogeneous particles is that he wrote "*homoe-omeries*" *prima manu* in Nos. 60 and 64, subsequently erasing the term in both entries, and substituting "Homogeneous particles" in No. 60 and "Homogeneous portions of matter" in No. 64. Whether Berkeley in making the erasure was simply adapting the spelling to contemporary usage in imitation of Bayle, or whether he did not wish to *identify* his conception with that of

* *Novum Organum*, I, 63.

Anaxagoras, does not matter; in either case there must have been some connection with the concept of Anaxagoras, which helped Berkeley in his difficulties about creation.

Anaxagoras opposed the mechanism of the Ionian physicists, and he used a subtle notion of composition that we should call *biological* or *organic* (see above, p. 70). He held that everything is made up of miniatures of itself, and that the seed of a tree is a little tree. Now ontogeny is supposed to recapitulate phylogeny, and phylogeny to anticipate ontogeny, and if the homogeneous particles were of the nature of genes or germs, we can see why Berkeley found them useful to contemplate, and thought of bringing them in to answer the objection of God's creating sun and plants etc. before animals. It is a mere point of theory; but it is of interest to see that Berkeley was moving away from his mentalism, and contemplating the creation of such non-mental things as homogeneous particles. Berkeley had by this time begun to see that his religion as well as his philosophy required the existence of the *other* of mind. Provided the things created before Adam are conceived as created in relation to mind, significant for mind, and preparatory for mind, and not as absolute existents, as matter is supposed to be, there is no substantial difference between Moses and Berkeley as to what happened "in the beginning".

Leaving Berkeley's Creation problems we pass on to the further developments in his doctrine of body evidenced in the *Commentaries*. These consist in a consolidation of the ground gained, a new stress on law and the course of nature, and the transition from doubt about the external world to certainty.

Consider the following group:

M   *The Reverse of ye Principle introduc'd Scepticism.*

(No. 304)

M   *N.B. On my Principles there is a reality, there are things, there is a rerum Natura.*

(No. 305)

K

M   *4 Principles whereby to answer objections viz—*
        1. Bodies do really exist tho' not perceiv'd by us.
        2. There is a law or course of Nature.
        *3. Language & knowlege are all about ideas, words
        stand for nothing else.*
        *4. Nothing can be a proof against one side of a con-
        tradiction that bears equally hard upon the other.*
                                            (No. 312)

The "Reverse" of the Principle is *esse est non-percipi*; it is mentioned again in No. 411, where again it is stated to have been the
main source of scepticism; for if real things were in a state of
absolute non-perception, we could never be sure that we are in
contact with reality. In discovering the Principle, Berkeley
discovered, he thought, the cure for scepticism, and doctrinal
changes followed. In the above group the reader will notice the
strengthening and broadening of the notion of body. Bodies
are realities, and not appearances; they are "things", not aspects; they are not isolated phenomena, but integrated in the
fabric and course of nature, and they are subject to nature's
laws.

On the last page but one of notebook B Berkeley takes stock,
and draws out the balance-sheet of his immaterialism (No.
391). Philosophers lose their Matter. Mathematicians lose their
insensible sensations. The profane lose their extended Deity.
The rest of mankind lose nothing, "as for bodies &c we have
them still."

In notebook A the entries on body are the following: Nos.
405, 408, 427, 429, 461, 472, 473, 474, 474a, 477, 477a, 493,
517, 517a, 518, 535, 546, 546a, 550, 686, 686a, 777, 800, 801,
802, 863 and 882. It is a long list that contains interesting
points of detail, but represents no major change in doctrine.
The position taken up at the end of notebook B is the starting-
point of notebook A (Nos. 405, 408) and also its conclusion
(Nos. 863, 882).

Common sense is now the key-note:

M.P.   *All things in the Scripture wch side with the Vulgar against the Learned side with me also. I side in all things with the Mob.*

(No. 405)

M.E.   *I must be very particular in explaining wt is meant by things existing in Houses, chambers, fields, caves etc wn not perceiv'd as well as wn perceiv'd. & shew how the Vulgar notion agrees with mine when we narrowly inspect into the meaning & definition of the word Existence wch is no simple idea distinct from perceiving & being perceiv'd.*

(No. 408)

Berkeley sides with the vulgar about body, because the vulgar side with him. The vulgar do not believe in material substance; they do not believe that our percepts are copies of material things. They believe that we see and touch real things, and that what we see and touch are real things. Berkeley gives instances in Nos. 427, 427a and 429. We see the horse itself, the church itself, and the books themselves; they are *ideas*, immediate objects of sense "and nothing more"; there is no absolute or material horse or church or book over and above the horse, church and book we see and touch. Berkeley and the vulgar are at one on that point. Do these things exist? Yes, of course; they are perceived; they are seen and touched. Now lock up the horse in the stable and the books in the study, and forget the church. Do they continue to exist? Yes, of course; why not? They can be perceived, they can be seen and touched; of course they continue to exist, as every Tom, Dick and Harry knows. Their *esse* is *percipi*, or *posse percipi*. "The horse is in the stable; the books are in the study, as before."

These striking declarations are made the more striking by their background of denial, doubt, hesitation and compromise, and by their position at the opening of the new notebook. They are the first-fruits of the revision; they form the foundation stone of the *Principles*; they bid farewell to Berkeley's first arguings, and endorse his second thoughts.

Nos. 461 and 493 should be read in connection with the *powers* theory of body. When he wrote them Berkeley had come round to see that Locke's simple idea of power is not simple, but is a compound of cause and effect. The consequent resolving of the power into cause and effect ended the original *powers* theory. Berkeley now realized that the body was not the power, but its effect.

Nos. 472 and 473 are continuous and in dialogue form, and I will take the liberty of expanding them into a dialogue in order to bring out Berkeley's two rather subtle points, which readers sometimes miss. Berkeley is on *imagined* existence,* and he makes two points about it, viz. (1) imagined existence is existence imagined perceived or perceivable, and (2) not all imagined existence is imaginary. The following imitation tries to illustrate these two points:

HYLAS.   Well met, Philonous; I was on my way to your house.

PHILONOUS.   Good morrow, Hylas. I am at your service. Can I do anything for you?

HYLAS.   Yes, Philonous; I was coming to borrow your *Malebranche*. I want to read that Illustration of which you were speaking yesterday. Would you be so good as to lend it to me?

PHILONOUS.   With the greatest of pleasure. Come back with me now, and collect it. It is on my study table.

HYLAS.   You speak confidently, my philosopher friend. Are you quite sure it is there?

PHILONOUS.   Well, tolerably sure, Hylas, though Bayle says we can't be sure of anything. I left it there five minutes ago, and locked the door.

HYLAS.   You locked the door. Then there's no one there to see it. It is not being perceived, and it does not exist, if its *esse* is *percipi*, as you are always preaching.

* cf. No. 777, and see *Principles*, section 23.

PHILONOUS. Hold there, good Hylas. True, the book is not being perceived at this moment by man; but it can be perceived; it is visible, tangible, perceivable; it is not imperceptible, like the matter from which you take your name. It is always in relation to perception, and is never out of it. Come along; we haven't far to go. I'll unlock the door, and let you see it for yourself, and touch it, and take it away.

HYLAS. Pardon me, Philonous, for saying so; but that is not the point, is it? I am reasonably sure I shall see it and touch it when we get there. It will exist *then*. I will take your word for *that*. But what about *now*? That is the point. Does it exist *now*?

PHILONOUS. Yes, Hylas; I should say it exists *now*. It could not be perceived then, if it were not perceivable now. And to be perceivable now, it must exist now.

HYLAS. You say it exists *now*. Then you are imagining the book to exist when it is not being actually perceived by the senses, are you not?

PHILONOUS. I am.

HYLAS. At this moment then you are imagining your *Malebranche* on your study table; and it is an imaginary copy of the *Recherche* you are going to lend me. On these principles of yours, things have only an imaginary existence between perceivings; and there are no real bodies that exist during the gaps in perception, and there is no solid difference between appearance and reality. See what comes of scrapping matter!

PHILONOUS. Not so fast, my real and sensible friend. *Distinguo*. I make a distinction. There are different types of existence. Objects of sense exist, and objects of the imagination exist. Objects of sense are the more important for most folk in practical life, and sensible existence is graded No. 1, and is commonly regarded as the standard type; but objects imagined or conceived exist, too; or they could not be imagined or conceived. When necessary we

must recognize imagined existence and conceived existence, and we must not confuse either type with sensible
existence. To perceive by sense is one thing; to imagine is
another thing.

I left a real book, visible and tangible, on my study table.
You ask me whether it exists now. I answer, Yes. You
could not ask the question without in some shape or form
imagining the book; nor could I answer it without doing
likewise. The book has imagined existence. You and I in
question and answer imagine it visible, tangible, perceivable. We could not imagine it material; that would be to
imagine it unperceivable. The act of imagining does not
bring the book into *sensible* existence; books would be
cheap and easy to come by, if it did. Whether the *Malebranche* has, or has not, *sensible* existence depends on the
facts and the course of nature, and not on your imagination, or mine. None the less what is imagined is imagined
to exist, i.e. to be perceivable by sense.

HYLAS.   Then by the same token, if I ask a question about
a chimera, the chimera exists?

PHILONOUS.   Yes, certainly. In the sense of my previous
remark, the chimera exists. A chimera is an imaginary
creature, part lion, part goat, and part horse; lions, goats
and horses are perceivable by sense, and chimeras are
imagined perceivable by sense. There is no chimera to see
or touch or otherwise perceive by sense. The chimera has
not sensible existence, and no body claims that it has; but
it has imagined existence, and its existence is imagined
perceivable. The *esse* of the chimera is *imaginari*. You see,
my good friend, I use the word *existence* in a larger sense
than is customary.

(Expansion of Nos. 472–3)

The two entries, represented by the above dialogue, have
left their mark on section 23 of the *Principles*; neither in his
book or notebook does Berkeley say or imply that asking the

question or evoking the image brings the thing imagined into sensible existence. He implies the very opposite. His "books" are assumed to be real objects with sensible existence. His "chimera" is assumed to be an unreal object without sensible existence. Asking the question and evoking the image do not alter fundamental facts. We have the power of imagining, as we have the power of seeing; but the one power is not the other. We easily imagine "books existing in a closet, and no body by to perceive them"; but that does not mean that we can imagine the matter of the books or material books; such objects are as unimaginable, as they are imperceptible. We can imagine books and omit to imagine the observer; but that omission does not alter the fact that the imagined books are imagined observable.

We come now to five entries which comment on the scholastic distinction between *ens reale* and *ens rationis*. Berkeley hesitates about it, contradicts himself about it, and makes it look more important than it really is (Nos. 474, 474a, 535, 546, 546a); he calls it a foolish distinction (No. 546), and yet he maintains it (No. 474a). It is a foolish distinction, if *ens reale* be taken to mean matter; if not, not. The books seen, like the books imagined, "solum habent esse in intellectu" (No. 474); for all *esse* is within the compass and range of mind; on that score there is no difference between *ens reale* and *ens rationis*. There is a world of difference, of course, between an imaginary thing, like a chimera, that cannot be seen and touched, and a real thing, like a book, that can. The *esse* of both types is to be in relation to mind, whether it be mind-imagining or mind-perceiving. The two types have that in common; in other respects they are poles apart.

It has become clear that the correct interpretation of Berkeley's immaterialism hinges on the distinction between material body which he denied and sensible body which he affirmed. We can see him coming gradually to full awareness and acceptance of it. He draws the distinction clearly in Nos. 477, 477a, 517, 517a, 518 and 550. I will print the first two, as they appear in the manuscript; they explain themselves, and need no comment:

	(verso)		(recto)
M	*or rather why he sup-poses all ys Matter, for bodies & their qualitys I do allow to exist independently of Our mind.*	M	*Ask a man I mean a Cartesian why he sup-poses this vast struc-ture, this compages of Bodies. he shall be at a stand, he'll not have One word to say. wch sufficiently shews the folly of the hypothesis:*
	(No. 477a)		(No. 477)

Berkeley is quite clear about the difference between sensible things and matter; he comments on the realism of his own approach to externality (Nos. 517, 517a, 518), declares that he takes away nothing that is real, and that he will stress and illustrate the reality of things and the course of nature (No. 550).

A long silence about body followed, and Berkeley was occupied in re-shaping his doctrine of mind; then in No. 686 he cast his mind back to Malebranche and the excursus on the difficulty of proving the existence of body; and opposite it on the facing page he wrote that remarkable entry, already quoted (above, p. 131), about his second thoughts on body. In effect he says, "I used to think Malebranche right about body; now I know he is wrong. I myself have gone from one extreme to the other. I used to be certain that body did not exist; now I am sure it does."

Berkeley went on to examine the psychology of certainty, and in the following entry,* which for pith and brevity could hardly be bettered, he puts the case in a nutshell:

* Note that it is marked "S" for "Soul-Spirit", not "M" like most of those on *body*. Berkeley is on the psychological element in our apprehension of body.

S   *To be sure or certain of wt we do not actually perceive*
     (I say perceive not imagine) We must not be altogether
     Passive, there must be a disposition to act, there must be
     assent, wch is active, nay wt do I talk There must be
     Actual Volition:

                                                    (No. 777)

How can a man be sure of the existence of the perceivable (as
distinct from the imaginary)? He is looking at the table top at
the moment; how can he be sure the bottom side is there, and
is not imaginary? Berkeley answers, By having a disposition to
act and doing incipient actions, such as putting out the hand to
touch the other parts of the table, which are hidden from sight.
Berkeley does not say that our disposition to touch the other
parts of the table, for instance, brings them into existence. He
is not on *existence* here, but on *certainty*. He simply states the
undeniable fact that our disposition and will to see and touch
what we are not actually seeing and touching gives us the
assurance that it is there to see and touch.

We must glance now at three consecutive entries that final-
ize and clinch the results of the long debate on body. All three
have been quoted before separately to illustrate other points;
all three should be read together here as a summary expression
of the teaching of the *Principles* on the existence of body:

M.P.E. *Malbranch in his Illustration differs widely from me He*
        doubts of the existence of Bodies I doubt not in the least
        of this.

                                                    (No. 800)

P   *I differ from the Cartesians in that I make extension,*
        Colour etc to exist really in Bodies & independent of Our
        Mind. All ys carefully & lucidly to be set forth.

                                                    (No. 801)

M.P   *Not to mention the Combinations of Powers but to say the*
        things the effects themselves to really exist even wn not
        actually perceiv'd but still with relation to perception.

                                                    (No. 802)

In No. 800 Berkeley repeats what he had said previously (Nos. 686, 686a) about Malebranche's doubts and his own certainty. The collocation of the marginal letters "M.P.E." occurs nowhere else. It indicates the key position of this argument. "M" stands for immaterialism, the general theme; "P" stands for the primary and secondary qualities—the basic argument of the first arguings; "E" for Existence indicates the new Principle which superseded the original line of argument. In No. 801 Berkeley again distinguishes his teaching from that of the Cartesians, and asserts the real and independent existence of the qualities of body, both primary and secondary. Finally (No. 802) is registered the formal decision not to mention the combination of powers, the mainspring of the original theory of body, and the focus of the greater part of the discussion. He will not mention these powers. He has shelved the theory; he does not deny it or refute it, but corrects it, and for fear of misunderstanding leaves it aside. The combinations of powers are not mentioned at all in the *Principles*. Powers in a powerful Spirit appear in one passage in the third Dialogue* to prove the existence of spirit; but of course the divine powers that cause, continue, sustain and move body are very different from the divine powers that originally were alleged to *be* body.

What then *are* bodies for the Berkeley of the *Principles*? They are "the things the effects themselves", which we perceive by sense, which really exist and are still perceivable, even when not actually perceived by man. They are "still with relation to perception". This pregnant phrase, which has not yet received the notice it deserves, is the key term of Berkeley's revised immaterialism; it is broad, elastic and yet decisive; no matter how far we men push research in the macroscopic world by observation, or in the worlds of the microscope and telescope by thought and imagination, we shall never come on anything not in relation to perception; we shall never come on matter; we shall never have reason to suspect the existence of anything

* *Works*, Vol. II, pp. 239–40.

neutral to mind and spirit, or of anything to which mind and spirit are neutral.

The revised conception of body entailed the revision of the concept of mind which is analysed in the next chapter; and fittingly Berkeley's last two statements about body in his notebooks speak of it in connection with mind. They are:

M.S. *Bodies exist without the Mind i.e. are not the Mind, but distinct from it. This I allow, the Mind being altogether different therefrom.*

(No. 863)

M.P. *I will grant you that extension, Colour etc may be said to be without the Mind in a double respect i.e. as independent of our Will & as distinct from the Mind.*

(No. 882)

In conclusion I will summarize the stages of development of the notion of body, covered in the present chapter. When in the summer of 1707 Berkeley came back to his thesis on immaterialism after his election to a Fellowship, he realized the danger of scepticism, and decided that he must assert the existence of body, and he did so throughout the earlier portion of notebook B by aid of a tactical refinement, not far removed from a quibble. Bodies exist, he said; but their existence is not actual; they exist as combinations of powers in God. Three lines of thought shook that position and led to its abandonment. It is clearly wrong to identify body with the power or powers behind it. Again, the notion of power is composite; it involves the relation between cause and effect. The cause cannot *be* its effect, and the *powers* theory runs the two together in an impossible way. Thirdly, the discovery of the Principle and of the meaning of the term *exist* put a new face on the problem. Berkeley found he could reject matter without rejecting the sensible. The crisis came with the attempted recognition of two meanings of the term *body* in connection with the problem of the Mosaic account of Creation. Berkeley realized that a pre-Adamite creation necessitated body as a collection of thought-things, as distinct from a collection or combination of powers. Notebook A consolidated that position by building body into the concept of nature, subject to law and in agreement with common sense, by recognizing and explaining imagined existence and distinguishing it from real existence, and explaining the psychological basis of certainty about the perceived and the perceivable. In the end the combinations of powers were shelved, the real world of sensible things was contrasted with the supposed world of insensible matter, and mind and body were recognized as in mutual relation, but yet altogether different the one from the other.

CHAPTER X

PERSON, CONSCIOUSNESS AND MIND

BERKELEY had second thoughts on mind, too. In the present
chapter we shall meet striking changes in his doctrine and
terminology of spirit; person and consciousness fade out, and
distinct mind emerges; in consequence *idea* replaces *thought* as
the term of precision for the object of sense. Ideas of spirit are
rejected. The activity of mind is stressed. The will rises to
psychological primacy, and finally the notion of mind is fixed
as the concrete of will and understanding. All these developments will be traced in the notebooks, and we shall add a
discussion on the intermittency of Berkeleian mind.

Berkeley's changed outlook on body and the external world
reacted sharply and soon upon his views on person, consciousness and mind. The distribution of entries shows it. The notebooks contain in all 132 entries marked "S" for "Soul-Spirit";
of these 12 entries are in notebook B and 120 in notebook A.
There is no sustained discussion of psychological questions,
arising from immaterialism, in notebook B;* in notebook A, on
the other hand, psychological questions arising from the revision begin as soon as Berkeley gets fairly under way, and they
increase in number and deepen in penetration as the work
proceeds. After his opening survey of the new situation and a
few notes on infinitesimals for his paper "Of Infinites",†

* Free-will and necessity are discussed in Nos. 145, 145a, 146, 149, 155,
166 and 357; Nos. 176 and 176a are on the metaphorical character of
speech; Nos. 84, 194a and 230 touch, respectively, on the *powers* theory,
personal identity and ideational knowledge of the soul. In Nos. 34, 96 and
121 the "S" should have been erased; it belongs to an earlier usage, see
above, p. 57.

† Read before the Dublin Philosophical Society on 19 November 1707,
and important for the dating of the notebooks; see above, p. 44.

157

Berkeley plunged into the psychology of his revised immaterialism with the searching query:

S   *Qu: how is the soul distinguish'd from its' ideas?*
certainly if there were no sensible ideas there could be no
soul, no perception, remembrance, love, fear etc. no
faculty could be exerted.

(No. 478)

This entry, as the "Qu:" may indicate, marks the opening of a new line of study. At an earlier stage Berkeley could hardly have asked that question, and certainly could not have made those statements; but now he can do both; for he recognizes a real subject, a real object, and a real distinction between them. If there were no sensible ideas, there could be no soul. It is a strong statement, and the remarkable phrase "sensible ideas" occurs here for the first time. I commented above (p. 31) on the appearance of the phrase in the *Principles*; here I must note its significance in the notebook. Berkeley uses it again in No. 544. Visible and tangible ideas have been mentioned several times already. Sensible things, bodies, qualities and objects are accepted. In other ways, too, Berkeley makes it plain that his ideas of sense are sensible, notably by distinguishing them from ideas of the imagination. The appearance of the generalized term "sensible ideas" in No. 478 at the outset of his study of distinct mind is Berkeley's recognition that man's mental life without a world of sense would be impossible. He could not have used it consistently at the earlier stage when he held that only mind existed. But now he is beginning his process of changing ideas into things without changing things into ideas.* Objects in necessary relation to mind are *ideas*. Objects that can be seen, touched and otherwise perceived by sense are *things*. Berkeleian ideas of sense are therefore idea-things, sensible ideas. Such ideas, collected and named and observed to go together "constitute . . . sensible things".† Ideas that

* *Works*, Vol. II, p. 244.
† *Principles*, section 1.

constitute sensible things are in principle *sensible*. Berkeley's *collections* of sensible ideas were precipitated from his *collections* or *combinations* of powers in God; and his use of the phrase *sensible ideas* in this entry crystallizes the results of the revision, and commits him to a structural alteration in his metaphysic and to an adjustment in his *psychology*; for the distinct existence of sensible ideas requires the distinct existence of percipient mind.

Distinct mind or soul was a difficult question for Berkeley because of his previous commitments, and he spent weeks and months on it; and from it radiate most of the psychological questions discussed in notebook A. Is the soul a substance? Is "the passing thought the only thinker"? Can the soul be known? If so, how? Is there an idea of the soul? What are the parts of the soul, and which is primary?

Berkeley began the *Commentaries* with the curious notion of an immortal person with a mortal soul. The immortality of the soul, he wrote, is not necessary "for ought we can see" (No. 14). It was a strange statement from a candidate for Holy Orders, who preached an orthodox sermon, still extant, on Life and Immortality* a week or two after making this entry, and who offered a demonstration of the natural immortality of the soul in the Preface of the *Principles* and sketched it in section 141. Berkeley's terminology was fluid at the time, and he could be unconcerned about the soul, because behind and above it stood a mysterious thing called the person, the bearer of immortality (No. 14) and the sole real existent. He wrote:

+   *Nothing properly but persons i.e. conscious things do exist, all other things are not so much existences as manners of ye existence of persons.*

(No. 24)

It is an amazing statement, utterly wild and irresponsible and untrue; but quite frank and unambiguous. "He couldn't have meant it"—we say to ourselves; but he did mean it, or he had

* On 11 January 1708; see *Works*, Vol. VII, p. 9.

meant it. He may have begun to have doubts about it when he set it down here for examination along with the tenets of his first arguings; but there it is in Berkeley's handwriting*—a towering statement about heaven and earth, mind, body and all that is. Other entries confirm its substance.

I discussed it above (p. 82) as the climax of his unrevised immaterialism and the starting-point of the revision. Here I must deal with the psychology behind it. Only persons exist. Only conscious things exist. The statements are so unnatural and bizarre and paradoxical that an explanation is called for. We may rule out the traditional explanation that there was some kink in the man. There was none. He was a sane, level-headed man, shrewd, sober and modest. He was a soldier's son; his eyes looked their own height, and his feet were firmly set on *terra firma*. He suspected zeal and regarded enthusiasm as a sin. His balance of mind, intellectual integrity and critical acumen are in evidence on page after page of his notebooks.

Only persons exist. Only conscious things exist. These paradoxes were the logical outcome of Malebranche's method of disproving rational evidence for the existence of material body. Bring the secondary qualities, he said, into the mind one by one; they are only modes of mind. Simon Foucher† added, "bring the primary qualities one by one into the mind". Where then is the evidence for the existence of the material body of the wax? Its colour, smell, sound, texture and temperature are in the mind. Its size and shape, motion and rest are in the mind. What then is left of the supposed matter or body of the wax? Nothing. Nothing is left outside the mind in matter. There is no material wax or body. Apply the same reasoning to sun, moon and stars, to mountains and rivers, to earth, air, fire and water. What is left of them? Nothing. Nothing is left outside the mind. There is no matter or material substance. Nothing is left in the world of man but persons conscious of their thoughts. Nothing properly but persons, i.e. conscious things, exist. *Q.E.D.*

* See frontispiece, lines 17–19.
† See above, p. 71.

This method of arguing is referred to and sketched in sections 14 and 15 of the *Principles*, as noticed above (p. 46), where Berkeley contrasts his old line of argument with his new line. Modern philosophers, he says, prove the secondary qualities not to exist in matter or without the mind; and the same may be proved of all the other sensible qualities. Going through the list—hot, cold, colour, sweet, bitter, extension, figure and motion—Berkeley comments on the limitations of "this method of arguing" and contrasts it with "the arguments foregoing", which, in his view, completely disprove the existence of matter.

That passage from the *Principles*, read along with the notebooks and in the context of the revision of 1707–8, takes on a new significance. It is autobiography; it is a flash-back to the turning-point in the making of the *Principles*. When he had discovered his Principle, Berkeley could afford to criticize Malebranche and his method; before that discovery, not. Without his Principle he depended on Malebranche and his method for the lifeblood of his thesis, and his use of Malebranche is beyond dispute.

Now Malebranche, for all his guarded expressions and hypothetical method of arguing, was an extremist; he outdid "the modern philosophers"; for he made the secondary qualities *"modifications de l'âme"*. He went far beyond relativity and subjectivity, and stretched the phrase "in the mind" till it became equivalent to *mental*. Colour, for Malebranche, is not only relative to the observer; it is not only conditioned by the observing; it is actually part of the observer's soul or mind. Soul and mind are coloured. No wonder Berkeley took them to be mortal, too. For two or three years Berkeley worked at immaterialism under the influence of Malebranche and his "sublime notions". During that apprenticeship the paradoxes of entry No. 24 would come naturally to his lips. If the colour *red* and its extent or spread are literally modifications of the soul, what are they but manners of personal existence, modes of consciousness, as Berkeley in this entry declares them and all "other things" to be? Such statements offend against common

L

sense, as Berkeley eventually saw; but at an earlier stage before the revision, he certainly believed for a time that only persons or conscious things (properly speaking) exist, and he recorded that fact in the entry we are studying.

Against this background it is a striking fact that both the terms, person and consciousness, are virtually missing from his published works. He adopted them at the outset of his study, and later gave them up. He adopted them because he found them, and found them together, in Locke's Essay.* A person, Locke says, "is a thinking intelligent being, that has reason and reflection, and can consider itself as itself, the same thinking thing, in different times and places; which it does only by that consciousness which is inseparable from thinking." Locke placed the identity of the person in consciousness, not substance. Berkeley was not satisfied on that point, but otherwise he agreed with Locke about the *person*, and meant by the term what Locke meant, viz. a self-conscious thinking being.

In the *Commentaries* a good deal is said about the *person*. It is immortal (No. 14); it is completely known (Berkeley thinks, No. 25); it is affected by sensations (No. 36); it differs from will and desire (No. 142); persons not thinking are to be allowed a potential existence (No. 185); persons are the only identical individuals (No. 192); persons have will (No. 194a) and identity (No. 200); a person discovered the Principle (No. 285); the word *person* cannot stand for an idea (No. 523); there are no time-intervals in personal existence; each person's time is measured by his ideas (No. 590); finally, the person (Berkeley implies) is "the concrete of the will and understanding", but he will call that concrete *mind*, not *person*, "lest offence be given"; he will not define *person*, or make much mention of it (No. 713). Here Berkeley has the Trinitarian and Christological *formulae* in view (No. 715).

True to his word Berkeley dropped the term from his technical vocabulary. He used it here and there colloquially. He

* Book II, Chapter xxvii, especially section 9 on *personal identity* and the twenty sections that follow. Entries Nos. 200 and 202 refer to this discussion.

calls himself "an obscure person" in the Dedication of the *Principles*; he appeals to "any reasonable person" (sect. 20), and to "any considering person" (sect. 154) and Newton is "that extraordinary person" (sect. 110, 1st ed.). In a word he kept the term for use in practical affairs of life; but dropped it almost completely from his philosophy.*

This striking change could hardly have been made for prudential reasons only. Locke managed to say a great deal about *person* without giving much offence to theologians. The term *person* is too unitary and too self-contained to fit well into Berkeley's *revised* philosophy; *mind* had begun to supersede it long before he recorded his resolve to give it up.† I incline to think that the fear of giving offence to ecclesiastics only clinched a decision, already taken on other grounds. In other words I think that the abandonment of the term *person* was consequential on his abandonment of panpsychism.

At the same time, too, he abandoned his alternative to *person*, viz. *conscious thing*. No theologian could find fault with that term; Berkeley could have fallen back on *it* if he discarded its alternative for prudential reasons only. Berkeley spoke fluently the language of consciousness. He knew the term and its cognates well and he used them technically. He was familiar with Locke's long discussion on consciousness and unconsciousness, and he refers to the passage in Nos. 200 and 202. Three more entries use the term. In No. 578 Berkeley notes that consciousness, perception and existence of ideas are all one; in No. 681 he proposes a solution of Locke's difficulty about our supposed consciousness of actions we have not performed; and in No. 744 he declares that "all the volitions I am conscious to are mine". The language of consciousness came readily to his thought and his pen during his preparatory work; yet he never

* See also *Principles*, sections 100, 147, 148, and *Three Dialogues*, *Works*, Vol. II, pp. 169, 180, 237, 248. "A human spirit or person" (*Principles*, 148) is the only exception, I think.

† In the 200 entries preceding No. 713 *person* occurs twice only (Nos. 523, 590) and *mind* 11 times (Nos. 531, 539, 579, 580, 581, 603, 629, 651, 663, 667, 692).

once uses the substantive in either the *Principles* or the *Three Dialogues*. The adjective *conscious* occurs in section 155 of the *Principles* and in the *Three Dialogues* (*Works*, Vol. II, pp. 233–4). In both those passages it is used in its rich and proper sense of *joint* knowledge, and not in its reduced sense. In the former passage God is spoken of as "present and conscious to our inmost thoughts"; in the latter passage spirit and matter are contrasted; neither is known *qua object* or *idea*; we are conscious of our spirits; we are not conscious of matter.

The broad fact is that *persons* and *conscious things*, the sole real existents that Berkeley recognized in the summer of 1707, virtually passed out of his philosophic ken a year later, and were both replaced by *mind*. The change of terms was a symptom of a change of doctrine. His original immaterialism hinged on the notion of personal consciousness; his revised and published doctrine hinges on that of distinct mind.

Where lies the difference? One finds out by taking examples. The apple, stone, tree and book, says Berkeley at the opening of the *Principles*, exist in the mind; for they are perceived by the mind. That is good sense, though explanations and distinctions may be needed. To say that they exist in the person does not make sense, no matter what explanations and distinctions are offered. Can one say that they exist in *consciousness*? No; unless we are using that term in a weak and watery sense. We are not, strictly speaking, *conscious* of apples, stones, trees and books. We mind them; we bear them in mind; we think of them; but strictly, we are not conscious of them. A man is conscious of his aims and anger, but not of his apple; he is conscious of his headache, but not of his hat. His headache is for the time being part of himself; it is a mode of his being. He has to *mind* his hat in a high wind; but if in any sense he is conscious of his hat, the hat must be very old and battered or in the very latest style, and the man is really conscious of himself as wearing the hat and looking ill or well in it. Consciousness and self-consciousness tend to merge and become synonyms. Consciousness surrounds, enfolds and assimilates its object, and becomes one with it, as the man is one with the pleasure or pain he feels. *Consciousness* is *le mot juste* for panpsychist epistemology. *Mind* is different. Mind keeps its distance. Mind keeps its object at arms' length. Mind is aimed at its object, as the gun at its mark. The mind in perceiving and knowing makes contact like a well-aimed shot; but mind and its object remain distinct, however close they come. The object minded is in the mind, but not of the mind; it is for the mind, but not mental. The language of distinct mind is therefore out of place in a panpsychist system, and is exactly expressive of Berkeley's revised attitude towards objectivity and the external world.

When in the summer of 1707 Berkeley declared that only conscious things exist, he found no difficulty in declaring that all "other things" are modes of personal being. A year later he spoke a different language:

M.S.   *Bodies exist without the Mind i.e. are not the Mind, but distinct from it. This I allow, the Mind being altogether different therefrom.*

(No. 863)

Note the collocation "M.S." in the margin. Berkeley does not often bring them together. He does so because he is making a statement about both subject and object. No longer a panpsychist, he had accepted sensible body external to the human mind, and independent of it. He had changed his mind about body; he needs must change his language about the mind. As a result after months of careful reflection he penned and published the decisive statement, "This perceiving active being is what I call *mind, spirit, soul* or *my self.* By which words I do not denote any one of my ideas, but a thing entirely distinct from them."*
That was his official description by which his philosophy of mind must be judged. Every term in that description had been analysed in a cool hour by one who had made himself an expert epistemologist. He had outgrown the rapture of intellectual

* *Principles*, section 2.

discovery; he was well aware of the pitfalls on the right hand and the left. He knew exactly what he wanted to say, and he said it with ease and clarity. He has to describe "the perceiving active being", the correlate of the world of sense and of the thing of sense. He describes it first and foremost as *mind*, and he offers three alternative terms to cover its varying aspects and to suit its different contexts; but in all cases, whatever the aspect, whatever the context, this active being, this mind is "a thing entirely distinct" from its ideas. Nothing could be said more plainly. No realism could be more realist.

In the fifth Objection* the epistemological crux is brought into clear light; it is a subtle objection, and in answering it Berkeley picks his way from height to height sure-footed as a chamois. If extension and figure exist only in the mind, says the Objector, then the mind is extended and figured; the mind is large, small, straight and crooked. Berkeley replies, You might as well argue that minds are red, blue and green, because colours exist only in the mind, as all modern philosophers admit. This telling rejoinder spot-lights the point at issue and then Berkeley explains quietly and patiently exactly what "in the mind" in his system means and does not mean. He makes it clear that qualities of things are qualities of things and not qualities of minds. They are "in the mind", not as modes or attributes, but as *ideas*, i.e. as objects minded. Attributes, such as *thoughtful* and *brave*, qualify the mind that is thoughtful and brave; they are in the mind in one sense. Apples, trees, stones and books are "in the mind" in a very different sense; they do not qualify the mind; they are in the mind as *ideas*. The precise formula for objects in Berkeleian epistemology is that they are in the mind "only as they are perceived by it, that is, not by way of *mode* or *attribute*, but only by way of *idea*".

Thus the key term "in the mind" changed its meaning during the revision. During his Malebranchian days Berkeley conceived its sensible contents as homogeneous with the mind, and "in the mind" as Monday and Tuesday are in the week. After

* *Principles*, section 49.

the revision all that was changed. Mind and its contents are heterogeneous; they belong to different *genera*, the one active, the other passive. Things of sense are "in the mind" only as they are perceived by it; they are not modes or attributes of mind; they are entirely distinct from it. The conception of non-mental, sensible objects "in the mind" because perceived by the mind is fundamental in Berkeley's revised and published immaterialism.

Stress on the activity of mind marks notebook A, and as this stress increased, the distinction between mind and its ideas grew sharper and hardened off. Berkeley had no longer to ask himself what the difference was; he saw it at a glance; mind is active; ideas are passive. They are heterogeneous, and have nothing in common but the name *thing* or *being*.* The relation between them is preserved, of course; the philosophy hinges on that relation; the mind is for the idea, and the idea is for the mind. Minds exist to perceive; ideas exist to be perceived. *Distinct* is a better term than *different* on that account; but distinct or different the mind is not its ideas; its ideas are not the mind. Berkeley's sea has found its shore. The person conscious of purely personal experiences, aware of nothing but modifications of the self and modes of personal being, has made way for active mind confronting a passive world of sensible things. This is the second aspect of his return home after his intellectual odyssey. He has come back where he was before; he has come back to the common-sense dualism of the ordinary man, to his sober philosophy of sense and spirit without matter.

We must now discuss, with Berkeley, the *idea* of spirit. At first he accepted it, and during the revision he rejected it root and branch. The change fitted in well with his appropriation of the term *idea* for the passive object of sense; but it also reflects a deepening of the conception of spirit. He denied that a mental picture can truly represent our being and activity, or the being and activity of other spirits, finite or infinite. This denial set the seal of Berkeley's mature judgment on the distinctness of mind.

* *Principles*, section 89.

Mind and idea are so distinct, so different, so heterogeneous that the one cannot stand in for the other.

It began with Locke who laid it down as fundamental that, "We can have knowledge no farther than we have ideas."* At first Berkeley held this principle firmly, and he set it and its companion dogma about words as two axioms at the head of his "demonstration" of the Principle:

> *1. All significant words stand for Ideas*
> *2. All knowlege about our ideas*

(No. 378)

He set it down for examination:

M   *All knowlege onely about ideas. V.Locke B.4 c.1.*
(No. 522)

S   *It seems improper & liable to difficulties to make the Word Person stand for an Idea, or to make our selves Ideas or thinking things ideas.*

(No. 523)

Later he formally denied its truth:

Mo   *We may have certainty & knowlege without Ideas.*
(No. 730)

Berkeley had a difficult hand to play here, and he played it adroitly. Dogmatism built on the idea of God and the idea of the soul. Scepticism flowed from the denial of one or both. Berkeley sailed between Scylla and Charybdis. He had no use for the doctrinal subtleties of the Scholastics; but he could not allow it to be said that the Reverend George Berkeley, a pillar of the Church and a Bishop-to-be, did not believe in God or the soul. His position is this: We have a knowledge of God; we may be said to have a *notion* of Him in a large sense; but we have no idea of Him. We are aware of ourselves, of our minds, souls, wills and other activities; but we have no *idea* of any of

* *Essay*, IV, iii, 1.

these things, nor could have. Ideas are passive; spirits are active. Ideas of sense, ideas of the imagination—both types are out of place in speaking of active spirit. God, the soul, the mind and the will *ex hypothesi* are not objects of sense; mental images of them cannot be formed. Static pictures cannot convey the thrust and movement of dynamic realities. The opinion that they can do so became for Berkeley "the grand mistake":

S   *The grand Mistake is that we think we have Ideas of the Operations of our Minds. certainly this Metaphorical dress is an argument we have not.*

(No. 176a)

S   *The not distinguishing twixt Will & Ideas is a Grand Mistake wth Hobbs. He takes those things for nothing wch are not Ideas.*

(No. 806)

S.   *But the Grand Mistake is that we know not wt we mean by we or selves or mind etc. tis most sure & certain that our Ideas are distinct from the Mind i.e. the Will, the Spirit.*

(No. 847)

Berkeley's point is that we have no ideational knowledge of the *ego*, the self or the mind, and we fall into error if we think we have. Non-ideational knowledge of spirit, on the other hand, is the very hinge of much of the argument in notebook A. Berkeley was able to drop the two Lockeian principles from which he started, just because he discovered the emotive value of some words and the true type of our knowledge of spirits. In the *Principles*, too, the formal denial (sections 27, 135) of ideational knowledge of spirit is accompanied and qualified by equally strong assertions of non-ideational knowledge of spirit. We know spirit, he says, but not by idea.

Halfway through the *Commentaries* Berkeley altered his technical term for the object of sense from "thought" to "idea".

This was a highly significant change, another nail in the coffin of Berkeley's panpsychism. The reasons for the change are instructive. The term *thought* grew less and less appropriate as the mind grew more and more distinct, and more and more active. A *thought* is more properly an activity of the mind thinking than the passive thing thought, and mind is not always easy to distinguish from its thoughts; nor are *thoughts* readily distinguishable from the mind that thinks them.

In the earlier part of notebook B, viz. Nos. 164, 181, 194, 226 and 228, the objects of sense are described as "thoughts", and the usage was no accident; for in No. 194 where the manuscript reads "the existence of our thoughts (wch being combin'd make all substances)" Berkeley at first wrote "ideas" and then erased "ideas" and substituted "thoughts". The objects of sense are still "thoughts" in Nos. 280, 282, 293 and 299. No. 299 is the last occurrence of the usage, which does not occur in notebook A, the *Principles*, or the *Three Dialogues*.* Berkeley made the change soon after he discovered the Principle, and abandoned his *powers* theory of body. In the careful entry No. 280 *ideas*, *thoughts* and *perceptions* are equated, and on the following page he expresses his first doubts about his earlier usage (cf. Nos. 378 and 808):

+   *Thoughts do most properly signify or are mostly taken for the interior operations of the mind, wherein the mind is active, those yt obey not the acts of Volition, & in wch the mind is passive are more properly call'd sensations or perceptions, But yt is all a case.*

(No. 286)

As a term of precision for the object of sense *thought* will not do. It is not precise, and it blurs the distinction between the thinking and the thought. It came naturally to Berkeley's lips as long as he was a panpsychist, and doubted or denied the real existence of the world of sense; it helped him to maintain that

* It has survived in the *Essay on Vision*, section 41, as an alternative to "sensations" for objects of sight in a hypothetical case.

"other things" were modes of consciousness or personal being; but on discovering the Principle and converting to common sense, he scrapped it.

What should he put in its place? When Berkeley needed a term of precision applicable to all sensible objects in the perceptual situation, what term should he use? He experimented with *thing* for a short time. "I should perhaps have stuck to ye word thing . . .", he wrote (No. 807); and in No. 657a he notes that properly speaking the idea is a picture made by the imagination, and by contrast "the real idea" is the thing. He saw, however, the popularity of the term *idea* (No. 685), and realized that the insuperable objection to *thing* was its "latitude" (No. 644); it is freely applied to activities, like the will, to animate things, and in the Cartesian philosophy it was used technically of the thinking thing; and so after careful thought he decided in favour of *idea*.*

Berkeley was too good a stylist to be pedantic about it; he does not throw the word *idea* at his readers' heads *ad nauseam*; he has plenty of alternatives, adequate for descriptive purposes, such as thing, quality, object, sensation, perception; but when for doctrinal reasons he must indicate precisely the epistemic features, common to "a stone, a tree, a book and the like sensible things", he does so by styling them *ideas*.

His choice was correct. The idea, said Locke, is the object of thinking, and he gave a long list of examples of ideas, chosen from a wide area, viz. those expressed by the words, "whiteness, hardness, sweetness, thinking, motion, man, elephant, army, drunkenness."† Locke had given the term great vogue, and it would not have been easy for any writer on perception in those days to avoid it. True, Berkeley did not use it exactly in Locke's sense; but the two usages have a good deal in common; and Berkeley was entitled to the difference. After all the word *idea* by derivation is objective, and not subjective; to the Greek

* See Nos. 115, 369, 644, 657a, 685, 689, 757, 807, 872, and *Principles*, section 39.
† *Essay*, II, i, 1.

mind it meant a visual sketch or plan such as we actually see when we see a house; the use of it for a mental copy of a reality, or for an element in the cognitive process came much later. Besides Berkeley was a creative thinker with something new to say. His new wine needed new bottles. He did vary the popular usage, but only within reasonable limits. He did (in his own phrase) turn ideas into things, without turning things into ideas. He was fully entitled to do so. A master of thought is entitled to say, "By such and such a term I mean such and such a thing." The Berkeleian idea of sense is to be explained by the Berkeleian philosophy, not by the *ideas* of Tom and Dick and Harry. Immediacy, passivity, and intrinsic meaning or necessary relation to mind, characterize the Berkeleian idea. After giving his reasons in section 39 of the *Principles* for not adopting *thing* Berkeley adds, "Since therefore the objects of sense exist only in the mind, and are withal thoughtless and inactive, I chose to mark them by the word *idea*, which implies those properties."

The other main line of development is the rise of the will to primacy and the accompanying stress on the activity of mind and the passivity of the idea. Notebook B* contains little or no sustained discussion of psychological questions. The will is stated to be the only active power in No. 155, and two additions on the verso (176a and 362a) anticipate later discussions. In notebook A psychological discussion is full, sustained and directly concerned with immaterialism. Berkeley's attention to the will and activity was a consequence of his change of mind about the external world. Converted to the recognition of an immaterial world of sense, he saw it necessarily as a world of passive things without the power of the cause. The active-passive distinction grew sharper and sharper, and loomed larger

---

* In addition to the topics mentioned above (p. 162) the following topics come up for brief notice: the immortality of the soul or person, No. 14; the possibility of knowing the soul or person, Nos. 25, 154, 178 and 230; the essence and definition of the soul, No. 44; perception, as passive reception of ideas, No. 301.

and larger, and became the heart of the distinction between the mind and its ideas. Percipient mind is active; ideas perceived are passive.

In the *Commentaries* we can see Berkeley gradually building up to this position. He could not reach it all at once. In some contexts it is easy to see the mind as active; in other contexts, not. In constructive imagining the mind summons images from the vasty deep, shapes and re-shapes them, dismisses them and lets them go. In memory the mind recalls its past, searches its annals, explores the echoing corridors, and grows all hot and bothered till it finds what it seeks. The mind is certainly active. But then, what happens when we change our minds. 'I' change my mind. My mind does not change itself. It is passive; it is changed; and the mind that is changed, what is it but its contents—its thoughts, desires, feelings and percepts?

Clearly Berkeley had to do much hard thinking before he could rank as synonyms "mind, spirit, soul or my self". In No. 362a he proposes to take "the Mind for the Active thing wch I call I my self". The phrase "operations of the mind" occurs frequently (see Nos. 531, 544, 667); but he was a long time in fully conceding activity to the mind; and there was at least one remarkable period of relapse, when he penned that sceptical septet that Hume could have endorsed (Nos. 576–82). What is the soul (he asks) and what is the mind? "The very existence of ideas constitutes the soul" (No. 577), he replies, and "Mind is a congeries of perceptions" (No. 580). Both entries are obelized.

The will comes into prominence slowly but surely. Berkeley discusses the will, infinite and finite, as cause of change and spring of action; he discusses the will in relation to our cognitive and other powers. Locke's account of the will is considered in Nos. 145a, 357, 423, 598, 611, 616, 624, 626–8, 630, 653–4, 797 and 879. The views of Hobbes are noticed (Nos. 796–8, 806, 822), of Descartes (No. 798), of Malebranche (No. 107), and of William King (Nos. 142, 159). The will is the only active power (Nos. 131, 155); it is the spring of the operative powers, of inquiring and of judging (No. 166); it is considered in relation to perception and volition (Nos. 644–6, 674, 808, 815, 833). The will and the understanding are a very troublesome pair; they differ *toto coelo* (No. 643); they are distinct (Nos. 681, 708); they are united (Nos. 614a, 713, 812, 841, 848); they are identical (No. 854); they are abstract ideas, and, in abstraction, nothing at all (No. 871). These sudden and violent changes in part reflect changes in terminology; but they are also due to the hardening of the distinction between active and passive, and the fixing of spirit and ideas as the two heads of reality, known to men.

Volitions are discussed at length (see Nos. 615, 615a, 621, 635, 714, 788). The unity of the will is the substantial issue. At first Berkeley postulated an unknown substrate of volitions, and called it the will; later on he rejected this distinction, concluding that the will is everywhere the same, and that whether it be called one or many is a verbal point. Will is identified with soul in Nos. 478a and 814, and with pure spirit (Nos. 828–9, 847–8). The will is the seat of personal identity (No. 194a); it is the only causal power (Nos. 499, 699). The will is no abstraction (No. 867; cf. *Principles*, sect. 143). An idea of the will is emphatically rejected; see Nos. 657–9, 663, 665, 672, 684, 706, 756, 792, 828, 875 (also *Principles*, 135 ff. and above, p. 167, on ideas of mental activity in general).

The most important single entry on psychological matters is the following:

S   *The Concrete of the Will & understanding I must call*
      Mind not person . . .

                                                    (from No. 713)

Here Berkeley finally settles his terminology, abandons *person* and substitutes *mind*, and in his striking phrase "Concrete of the Will & understanding" registers the net result of the long discussion, and declares what he means by *mind*. Here he settles the terminology and the doctrine of his published works. With these words he leaves behind him the dangerous (as he

thought it) term *person* and the towering and really dangerous
personalism for which it had stood. The ground-plan of his
revised immaterialism is now complete. He has worked out his
Principle to its logical results; he has re-found body and the
world of sense; and for the abstract person or consciousness of
his first arguings he has substituted the distinct concrete mind
of his second thoughts.

"The concrete of the will and understanding"—the description is noteworthy. The Berkeleian *mind* is a concrete thing, as
concrete as George Berkeley himself; it is not a series of impressions or ideas, nor a congeries of perceptions, nor a bundle
of sensations. For my mind says "I"; my mind is "I, my self".
My mind is concrete, not of ideas and perceptions, but of will
and understanding. It is a terse, apt description of the philosophic mind, seeking truth; yet it is an unusual phrase, not in
the books. It looks like self-observation, and Berkeley may have
put himself on paper here, and given the formula of his own
spirit. For five long years he has examined the facts of the
perceptual situation, seeking the truth about the external
world. It has been a sustained course of high endeavour. Something concrete did it. Something concrete brought him day
after day, week after week, to his study table and his books and
notebooks. What did it? Who did it? Not a sensible body, not
a living organism, not a disembodied or lifeless spirit, but an
embodied, living mind, a perceiving active thing, George
Berkeley, who willed to understand.

The phrase answers reasonably well to the psychological
experience of the average man. We know ourselves to be a
concrete complex; we might wish to add an explicit recognition
of feeling and emotion; but on the whole we treat them as
secondary by-products of self-reference, and place first the
will to know. The will *per se* is a barren abstraction; and the
actual understanding is never a passive receptacle of knowledge;
and the two aspects of the mind do seem to grow together and
develop under the leadership of the will, and we may accept
Berkeley's description—"the concrete of the will and under-

standing" as adequate for all the main purposes of philosophic thought.

One psychological question remains. Does Berkeleian mind *continue* to exist? Or has it only an intermittent existence? It is not an easy question to ask, or to answer. Berkeley has not dealt with it very fully, nor answered it decisively; he has just let it die a natural death, as in practical life most of us do.

Without a doubt at some stage in his early thinking Berkeley held the intermittent existence of some important element in human personality, and changed his mind about it at a later stage. His doubt about the immortality of the soul (No. 14) must have had some connection with its intermittency; in fact he described intermittency as dying "oft in a day" (No. 83). From No. 185, quoted above (p. 137), we can see that the question of the existence of "persons not thinking" was a sister question to that of colours in the dark, and that at the time of writing Berkeley would not grant to such persons "an absolute actual existence"; and it should be noted that when at a later stage Berkeley commented on this entry on the facing page, he dealt with the colours in the dark, but made no reference to the persons not thinking. This omission is typical of Berkeley's attitude. He did not lose sight of the question, as we shall see; but he thought it of secondary importance. Similarly when he dealt with the intermittency of the object in the *Principles* (Section 48) and said that it and the companion doctrines do not follow from his principles, he said nothing at all about the intermittency of the subject. Probably he felt under no obligation to do so. There are difficulties in framing the question and ambiguities in the terms used. Berkeley has not tidied up the issue, and he has shown reserve about it, as he was entitled to do. By accepting concrete mind that wills and understands he secured the interests of common sense without prejudicing the *esse est percipere*, and *qua* immaterialist Berkeley was not further concerned.

Curiously enough Berkeley was questioned on this very point by a correspondent in America and the correspondence has survived.* His friend, Samuel Johnson, wrote to him about the *esse* of spirits, apparently hoping to elicit a declaration in favour of a soul-substance. Johnson writes, "Has a child no soul till it actually perceives? And is there not such a thing as sleeping without dreaming, or being in a *deliquium* without a thought? If there be, and yet at the same time the *esse* of a spirit be nothing else but its actual thinking, the soul must be dead during those intervals; and if ceasing or intermitting to think be the ceasing to be or death of the soul, it is many times and easily put to death. According to this tenet, it seems to me the soul may sleep on to the resurrection or rather may wake up in the resurrection state, the next moment after death."

Berkeley gave no specific reply to these questions. He pleaded haste; the ship carrying the mails was on the point of sailing. Besides I think he must have already discussed these questions at the study circles he conducted in Rhode Island which Johnson attended. In what Johnson says about the resurrection following the next moment to death, he is almost repeating Berkeley's words, and his phrases about the repeated death of the soul are curious echoes of the entry:

+   *Men die or are in a state of annihilation oft in a day.*
                                                    (No. 83)

Berkeley's reply "wrote in a hurry", traces Johnson's difficulties to the nature of time and the obscurity of language, and he adds, "In these matters every man is to think for himself, and speak as he finds. One of my earliest inquiries was about Time, which led me into several paradoxes that I did not think fit or necessary to publish, particularly the notion that the resurrection follows the next moment to death."

Berkeley laid aside his paradoxical speculations about annihilation and dying "oft in a day". The entry quoted above is obelized. The mind, like life, carries its own existence with it, for Berkeley, and Locke's mind that "thinketh not always"

* See *Works*, Vol. II, pp. 288 ff.

M

had no meaning for him. In Section 98 of the *Principles* Berkeley confesses to "odd thoughts of my existence" in consequence of hearing others talk of the infinite divisibility of time. He heartily disapproved of that doctrine, saying that it "lays one under an absolute necessity of thinking, either that he passes away innumerable ages without a thought, or else that he is annihilated every moment of his life: both which seem equally absurd."

If minds function intermittently, the problem of personal identity, always with us, becomes particularly acute. If a man dies oft in a day, and ceases to be when he ceases to think, and begins to be again when he again begins to think, is he the same person? Personal identity is discussed in Nos. 192, 194, 194a, 200 and 202; No. 201 obviously refers to table talk about it. The discussion is inconclusive; but the suggestion on the *verso* (No. 194a) that the will is the seat of personal identity is apparently accepted in No. 681—the only entry in notebook A to deal with it.

In his first letter to Johnson* Berkeley has some interesting speculations on "a change of state, such as is vulgarly called Death" in an immaterialist system. He knows they are speculations, and he speaks with the reserve that marks his whole treatment of the intermittency question; but about the basis of those speculations, viz. the existence of the world of sense, he shows no reserve at all. "It is sufficient for that purpose," he writes, "that we allow sensible bodies, i.e. such as are immediately perceived by sight and touch; the existence of which I am so far from questioning (as philosophers are used to do) that I establish it, I think, upon evident principles."

In 1729 when he wrote those words Berkeley believed in a world of sensible bodies, immediately perceived, and so he did twenty years earlier when he was doing the preparatory work for the *Principles*. He believed in the stable, continuing world of sense in which you and I believe. Once that position is reached, the sting is drawn from the problem of intermittency.

* *Works*, Vol. II, p. 282, section 6.

There can be no question of the natural order going in and out of existence with every turn of the observer's attention; nor of the observer ceasing to be when he ceases to observe. The only question is as to how the intermittency of our perceiving, and the obvious gaps in our seeing and touching square with the requirement that the mind always thinks. Berkeley has two answers, the one theoretical, the other practical. On the theoretical side he refers us, as he referred Johnson, to the difficulties of language and the nature of time. In entries Nos. 650, 651 and 652, he criticizes Locke for saying that thought is not essential to the mind; he asserts that it is a contradiction to say that the mind exists without thinking; he states that the mind always and constantly thinks, but that in sleep and trances it does not exist, because there is no succession of ideas in sleep and trances, and therefore no time. Even more explicit is the statement:

T   *No broken intervals of Death or Annihilation. Those intervals are nothing. Each Person's time being measured to him by his own Ideas.*

(No. 590)

Here Berkeley goes out of the frying-pan into the fire. In order to avoid saying "Our minds do not always think" he says in effect "Our minds do not always exist"; for when I am asleep I have no ideas; time is not, as far as I am concerned. In a word, he takes a private and personal view of time. This was only a temporary flight of fancy, an expedient not typical of his immaterialism or necessary to it. Time in the *Principles* (Sections 97, 98) is a common medium in which you and your servant meet; but it is not an absolute thing abstracted from the succession of ideas, "exclusive of all those particular actions and ideas that diversify the day".

In practice Berkeley solved this problem, as most of us do, by supposing a continuing disposition or faculty which operates intermittently. A perception, he says, "cannot exist without a thing to perceive it" (No. 280). *A thing to perceive it* is exactly a *faculty*, a thing designed and disposed to do what we are not always doing, like writing or lecturing. A perceiving subject is treated by Berkeley as having the faculty of sight, even when not actually seeing. *Faculty* language appears more than once in notebook A. If there were no sensible ideas, Berkeley says (No. 478), "no faculty could be exerted". He makes the penetrating remark that when the understanding is "taken for a faculty", it is not really distinct from the will (No. 614a), and in No. 777 "a disposition to act" is recognized as the guarantee of our certainty of the existence of sensible things.

The accent on the mind's activity in notebook A and the rise of the will to primacy bore directly on Berkeley's intermittency problem. When he was immersed in Locke's *Essay concerning Human Understanding*, the understanding and cognition naturally took first place with him, and he became acutely conscious of the gaps in our cognizing; but as he filled notebook A, he came to know himself better; the will took first place; the understanding dropped back; the gaps closed, and he became aware of the constant thrust of volitional life, pulsing through our whole mentality, and he wrote:

S.   *While I exist or have any Idea I am eternally, constantly willing, my acquiescing in the present State is willing.*
(No. 791)

Berkeley when he wrote those words must have ceased to think effectively of his mind as dying oft in a day and being many times re-born; he felt in himself the eternal will to live, and even acquiescence he accepted as unconscious willing. A few pages further on he wrote even more strongly to the same effect (No. 833); there are no ideas without will; there is no state of hedonic indifference; anything is preferable to annihilation. An intermittency, other than that of the intermittently acting faculty, is ruled out by those entries.

Thus before he had finished notebook A Berkeley had quietly dropped his earlier paradoxical views, and had come round to accept continuing active mind as the percipient subject and the seat of personal identity. With that development the doctrinal revision of 1707–8 was completed, the position of the *Principles* was reached, and Berkeley's immaterialism was in all essentials as we have it now. During the same period Berkeley felt his way to an adequate conception of the Infinite, with which we deal in the next chapter.

CHAPTER XI

GOD

In the earlier stages of the revision, if we may judge from the notebooks, Berkeley did not give specific thought to the nature of deity; he seems to have worked with the stock conception of the divine attributes, such as a thoughtful layman picks up from the general teaching of the Church. As the work progressed, however, he became more and more concerned with the philosophy of the subject; he felt the need of a conception of deity to match his metaphysic, large, lofty and rational. Towards the end of notebook A he found what he wanted; he compared his conception of deity with those of other philosophers, analysed and defined it, and laid down the lines of his own demonstration of the existence of God. The marginal sign system confirms this statement. Twenty entries have the marginal letter "G" for *God*; five of these occur in notebook B, and fifteen in notebook A, mostly towards the end; in addition there are some twenty more entries that refer incidentally to the being and nature of God. A definite advance can be traced; Berkeley's revised immaterialism required and received a revised conception of deity. Berkeley calls it a "discovery", calls it a great truth, lying near and obvious to the mind, but attained by the reason of very few, states its salient points, and sums it up in St. Paul's words, *In whom we live, and move, and have our being.**

This discovery completed the revision, and rounded it off. First Berkeley discovered the Principle; then he discovered real body and distinct mind, and lastly he discovered the *greatness* of God.

When at the outset of the revision Berkeley wrote that bodies *were* combinations of powers *in God*, had he given a thought,

* *Principles*, section 149. Section 6 should be read along with this passage.

one wonders, to the implications of the statement? Did the
term *God* mean to him at the time of writing more than the
asylum of human ignorance or the mystery in which the
avenues of speculative thought often end? If he had tried to
give a rational content to his words, he would have found himself supporting pantheism, or a corporeal deity. In point of
fact "God" was to him at the time "an unknown substratum"
(No. 80), and his phrase "in God" must have had little or no
positive content, like the pious "now with God" said glibly of
friends departed. Ten or twelve months later he had thought
things out, and had formed a very definite and positive conception of deity; for he declared that God is no blind agent,
that He possesses understanding and will, and that the properties of all things are in Him (No. 812).

This expansion and deepening of the notion of deity formed
an important part in the making of the *Principles* two hundred
and fifty years ago, and they are essential to a right understanding and just appreciation of the book today. To interpret
Berkeley's teaching about the world in terms of nursery or
Sunday school conceptions of God or those of adolescence, is
to send a boy on a man's errand. If we would take it and weigh
it seriously, we must think out Berkeley's metaphysic in terms
of a *great* God, immanent and transcendent: an immense,
eternal spirit, who embraces and encompasses the vastness of
space and all the long corridors of time, and who pervades and
animates the whole, as the life-force pervades and animates
evolution, as Shakespeare pervades and animates his creations,
and Picasso his pictures. In great writers the conception is
wont to rise with the theme; so it was with Virgil; so it was
with Berkeley. Virgil *used* the conventional deities of Olympus,
as poets did and do; but when he speaks his mind about
ultimate reality, Jupiter and Juno are left far behind, and it is
Spirit within that sustains the sky and earth and sea, the moon
and stars; it is *Mind*, that interfused throughout its members
moves the whole mass, and mingles with its mighty frame.*

* *Aeneid*, VI, pp. 724 ff.

Berkeley, too, can speak conventionally about God; but when he really speaks his mind, he writes as one who sees all things in God and God in all things. In Section 6, for instance, of the *Principles* he declares it to be a "near and obvious" truth that all the choir of heaven and furniture of the earth, viz. all those bodies which compose the mighty frame of the world subsist in the mind of some eternal spirit. The language is lofty, and it rings true. If there were no world of bodies, or if Berkeley did not believe in a world of bodies, such language would be indefensible, and it would ring false. And so what Berkeley solemnly declares to be a near and obvious truth is, for him, a truth about the world *and* a truth about God.

We all admit that the existence of the world is a near and obvious truth; the existence of God in Berkeley's system is just as near and obvious to the mind, if we have mastered that system, or entered into it. Here then is a touchstone of Berkeleian interpretation and a criterion of Berkeleian scholarship. In many expositions of Berkeley's teaching this truth is neither near nor obvious, and the Berkeleian deity is remote and odd. Berkeley's God is usually represented as an artefact, introduced like the *deus ex machina* of Greek drama in the last act to solve the insoluble problem. He is the *deus ex machina* for solving the problem of the unperceived perceivable, a device for keeping chairs and tables in existence over the gaps in human perception, and for preventing "the tree that I see from ceasing to be when there's no one about in the quad". How could the existence of a deity, so conceived, ever constitute a near and obvious truth? I suggest that there is a twofold mistake here. People mistake Berkeley's God for a cosmic conjurer, only because they mistake Berkeley's world for a cosmic illusion or mirage; but once they have grasped the fact that Berkeley's world of sense is as real as any realist could desire, then indeed the existence of Berkeley's God becomes a truth near and obvious to the mind, and in our reflective moments the very sight of the good green earth makes us think of God as naturally as the familiar handwriting of a letter makes us think of the friend that wrote it.

A real world of idea-things, distinct mind, and a great God —those are the three requirements of Berkeley's revised metaphysic of immaterialism. In previous chapters I have traced the development of the first two; I have now to deal with the third.

Greatness is a traditional attribute of God, covering the infinities of space, time and power. The *Oxford English Dictionary* quotes from Habington (1640), "Great God! When I consider thee, Omnipotent, Aeternall and Immense." Immensity was, at one time, a recognized divine attribute, correlated with eternity as is space with time. "It is repugnant to the immensity of God", wrote Bishop Stillingfleet.* Locke quotes from Solomon's prayer, "Heaven and the heavens of heavens cannot contain thee",† and adds, "God, every one easily allows, fills eternity; and it is hard to find a reason why any one should doubt that he likewise fills immensity." In the previous chapter (xiii, 27) he had raised the question without answering it, whether Solomon's words "or those more emphatical ones of the inspired philosopher, St. Paul, 'In him we live, move, and have our being,' are to be understood in a literal Sense". Berkeley knew both passages in Locke, and on folio 102 of notebook B he wrote the cryptic comment "God Space b.2, 13, 26, & 15.2". Berkeley was disturbed by the contemporary tendency among the mathematicians to make God extended (see Nos. 290, 298, 310, 391), and perhaps on that account he does not apply the term "immense" to deity, and uses the term "omnipresent" in its place.

The main scriptural authority for the divine omnipresence is St. Paul's dictum,‡ quoted above; this remarkable statement, covering more than omnipresence, was the central theme of the apostle's address to the philosophers of Athens on

* *Origines sacrae*, 1662, III, ii, 10.
† *Essay*, II, xv, 2, 3.
‡ Acts xvii, 28.

Mars Hill. At the cultural centre of the ancient world, in the very shadow of the Parthenon and looking down on the *agora* where Plato and Aristotle had taught, with spirit stirred within him, St. Paul delivered himself of this tremendous sentiment. He applied the words to organic life and its environment, to physical motion, and to the being of finite spirits. Berkeley applied it also to the bond of spirit, "that intercourse between spirits, whereby they are able to perceive the existence of each other".*

The text had a profound effect on Berkeley. He quotes it repeatedly at turning points in his argument, as we shall see. It supplied what his philosophy required, viz. the conception of a great universal spirit, embracing all space and time.

He mentions it first in connection with Spinoza, who in his 21st letter to Oldenburgh (quoted in the Preface of the *Opera Posthuma*, 1677) states, "Deum omnium rerum causam immanentem, ut aiunt, non vero transeuntem statuo. Omnia, inquam, in Deo esse, et in Deo moveri, cum Paulo affirmo." Oldenburgh, the secretary of the Royal Society, had written to Spinoza for a statement of his views; and this was part of Spinoza's reply. Berkeley refers to it in the following entry:

G.   *Spinosa (vid: Pref. oper: Posthum:) will Have God to be Omnium Rerum Causa immanens & to countenance this produces that of St. Paul, In him we live etc. Now this of St. Paul may be explained by my Doctrine as well as Spinosa's or Locke's or Hobbs' or Raphson's etc.*

(No. 827)

By this time Berkeley has so well thought out his doctrine, and is so clear as to the conception of God implied by it, that he can use his doctrine to explain "this of St. Paul", and of course very soon he will be using "this of St. Paul" to explain and defend his doctrine. The entry testifies to the young author's assurance and clear vision; but it has a strong polemical bias; for in effect he is charging Spinoza, Locke, Hobbes and

* *Principles*, section 147.

Raphson with giving a twist to St. Paul's words and using
them to justify their inadequate conceptions of deity. Raphson
came in for Berkeley's severest censure; for in his book *De
spatio reali seu ente infinito*, published in 1697, Raphson virtually
deified space, calling it "actus purus, incorporeum, immuta-
bile, aeternum, omni-continens, omnipenetrans, attributum
(viz. immensitas) primae causae" (Chapter V). Twenty years
later in his letter to Johnson of 24 March 1730 Berkeley referred
to Raphson as a mathematician who "pretends to find out
fifteen of the incommunicable attributes of God in space".

Berkeley's special interest in the Pauline text came to him
from Malebranche; at any rate he associated it specially with
Malebranche's doctrine of seeing all things in God. Malebranche in the central chapter of his *Recherche* (III, ii, 6) uses
St. Paul's words in a most impressive way, and makes them the
grand *finale* of his argument. At the climax of his argument in
the *Principles* (sections 148–9) Berkeley distinguishes his own
doctrine of "seeing" God from the "incomprehensible" doctrine
of Malebranche, and goes on at once to declare that there is
nothing more evident "than the existence of God, or a spirit
who is intimately present to our minds, producing in them all
that variety of ideas or sensations, which continually affect us,
on whom we have an absolute and entire dependence, in short,
in whom we live, and move, and have our being". In the second of the
*Three Dialogues** Berkeley again quotes the text, and again in
connection with Malebranche. He is distinguishing his views
from those of Malebranche; in effect he says in the first edition,
"I differ profoundly from Malebranche; but I agree with him
in holding that in God we live and move and have our being."
He quotes the text also in the third dialogue (p. 236), where he
is defending his use of the term *idea* for *thing*. Every unthinking
being, he says, "is necessarily, and from the very nature of
its existence, perceived by some mind: if not by any finite

* *Works*, II, p. 214. The passage should be read in the first edition; the
long addition in the second edition obscures the original sequence of
thought.

created mind, yet certainly by the infinite mind of God, in whom *we live, and move, and have our being*."

In the *Alciphron*, too, he quotes it, again at the climax of the metaphysical argument, again in connection with Malebranche. In the fourth dialogue, when the free-thinker has been put through the mill and has conceded the existence of God and his visual language, but "stares a little" at some conclusions, Euphranor says to him (Section 14):

> You, it seems, stare to find out that God is not far from every one of us; and that in Him we live, and move, and have our being. You, who, in the beginning of this morning's conference, thought it strange that God should leave Himself without a witness, do now think it strange the witness should be so full and clear?
>
> ALCIPHRON. I must own I do. I was aware, indeed, of a certain metaphysical hypothesis of our seeing all things in God by the union of the human soul with the intelligible substance of the Deity, which neither I, nor any one else could make sense of. But I never imagined it could be pretended that we saw God with our fleshly eyes as plain as we see any human person whatsoever, and that he daily speaks to our senses in a manifest and clear dialect.
>
> CRITO. As for that metaphysical hypothesis, I can make no more of it than you. But I think it plain this optic language hath a necessary connexion with knowledge, wisdom, and goodness. It is equivalent to a constant creation, betokening an immediate act of power and providence. It cannot be accounted for by mechanical principles, by atoms, attractions, or effluvia. The instantaneous production and reproduction of so many signs, combined, dissolved, transposed, diversified, and adapted to such an endless variety of purposes, ever shifting with the occasions and suited to them, being utterly inexplicable and unaccountable by the laws of motion, by chance, by fate, or the like blind principles, doth set forth and testify the immediate

operation of a spirit or thinking being; and not merely of a spirit, which every motion or gravitation may possibly infer, but of one wise, good, and provident Spirit, who directs and rules and governs the world.

Berkeley published the *Alciphron* in 1732; in the following year he published *The Theory of Vision Vindicated*, and on its title-page he set the words, In Him we live, and move, and have our being.

Berkeley's final conception of God as an omnipresent spirit, all-encompassing and all-penetrating, was no pious ornament of the system, but its very ground and foundation. He reached it and hammered it into shape while he was filling his notebooks and as a direct consequence of the revision. It was clinched for him and voiced by St. Paul's text. It is important in Berkeleian interpretation partly because it is Berkeley's own peculiar proof of the existence of God, and partly because it postulates and presupposes a world of sense, independent of our minds, and thus is a proof of Berkeley's genuine belief in the existence of that world. When he began the revision, he did not believe in the real existence of body; all was mind for him, and mind was all. At that stage there was nothing to call in question the nature of deity; but when Berkeley realized that a good God is no deceiver, and could not cause us to perceive things that are not there, he had to grant a real existence to the world of sense, independent of our minds, and then he had to expand and develop his conception of deity until the world's God *matched* God's world.

There are two demonstrations of the existence of God, mentioned in the *Commentaries*, and only two; one occurs near the beginning, and the other towards the end. The contrast between them is striking, and bears out the development traced above, in Berkeley's conception of deity. The earlier "demonstration" is vague and inconclusive; it smacks of *petitio principii*; the entry is marked with the obelus in the margin; it is a discarded entry. The later entry has the index letter "G" in the margin, and it contains a valid proof of the existence of God starting from the nature of the world as Berkeley saw it when he published the *Principles*. Here they are:

+   *Nothing corresponds to our primary ideas wthout but powers, hence a direct & brief demonstration of an active powerfull being distinct from us on whom we depend. etc.*

(No. 41)

G.   *Every sensation of mine wch happens in Consequence of the general, known Laws of nature & is from without i.e. independent of my Will demonstrates the Being of a God. i.e. of an unextended incorporeal Spirit wch is omniscient, omnipotent etc.*

(No. 838)

According to the earlier entry the existence of God is to be demonstrated from a negation, the absence of anything *without*, i.e. outside the mind. We have our primary ideas, extension, figure and motion; the course of the argument has shown that there is nothing *without* corresponding to them. *A fortiori* there is nothing *without* corresponding to colour, sound and smell and the other secondary ideas. There are no unconscious, unthinking things *without*. Yet we have a sense of *outness*; the great majority of our ideas are data, not self-originated, but external by origin, and they are forced on our notice as bodies. Therefore there must be a God, distinct from us. Berkeley intended his "demonstration" to proceed on some such lines. Unfortunately, however, at the time he penned that entry Berkeley was saddled with a panpsychist notion of body; he held that what we call *bodies* are in fact powers or combinations of powers in God to make us perceive them. His elaborate demonstration therefore boils down to a plain *petitio principii*. He takes for granted what he purports to demonstrate. There are powers in God; therefore there is a God. That is all he has really said. Apart from this formal flaw in the argument, there is a serious defect in substance. If Berkeley had stated it fully, it would run as follows: *There is no external world of body; yet we are irresistibly impelled to think there is; therefore there must be a powerful Being who makes us think so.* It is more like an argument for the existence of Descartes's all-powerful Demon, than for the existence of a good God. No argument of the sort appears in Berkeley's publications, and it is no wonder that the entry is marked with the obelus.

Turn to the other entry (No. 838), and we are in a different climate of thought, though the term *sensation* may hide the fact from hasty readers. A *sensation* in Berkeley's usage is not a subjective sensing, but an object sensed, an idea-thing. Such sensations constitute nature, and happen in accordance with the known laws of nature, and are independent of my will. Berkeley is measuring his words here, and writing with care. He is demonstrating the existence of God, not from subjective things like aches and pains, and dreams and stirrings of sense, but from objective things like the thunder-clap heard above the storm, the starry heavens seen on a frosty night, and the goodly smell of the vine in flower. Such things are obviously external and not material; they are significant reals, which we learn to understand and read as we read a book. When we read them as part of nature or the cosmic order, detached from the needs of practical life, the thoughtful mind can hardly fail to see in them a proof of the existence of a great Mind and Spirit, omnipresent, pervading, penetrating and encompassing.

In the earlier entry Berkeley tried to base his belief in God on the intermittent, momentary "bodies", potentially existing as combinations of powers in God; the attempt failed. In the later entry he bases his belief in God on the nature of sensible, continuing bodies, really existing independent of our wills; they cannot exist *in vacuo*; they are not minds, nor modes of mind; but they form the marvellous system of significant reals that we call the course of nature. This is not one of the traditional "proofs", but it is Berkeley's own; it has points in common with the argument from design. It is in effect a twofold demonstration; against the sceptics it establishes the world on sure foundations, as Berkeley more than once claimed; against atheists it establishes the existence of boundless spirit with power matching the marvels of man's perceptual life. This is the argument in which the *Principles* culminates; it is set forth in sections 146–9 with care and in fullness. The gist of it is in the following extract:

> "It is evident to every one, that those things which are called the works of Nature, that is, the far greater part of the ideas or sensations perceived by us, are not produced by, or dependent on, the wills of men. There is therefore some other spirit that causes them, since it is repugnant that they should subsist by themselves . . . whithersoever we direct our view, we do at all times and in all places perceive manifest tokens of the divinity: everything we see, hear, feel, or any wise perceive by sense, being a sign or effect of the Power of God . . . *in whom we live, and move, and have our being.*"

To complete the foregoing survey I must add some details about the entries on deity. In notebook B there are several notes on the God of traditional theology. Nos. 3 and 92 raise questions about the succession of ideas in the divine mind, conceived on the analogy of the human mind. No. 107 on "Man without God" reflects Malebranche's conception of God as the great Dynamic of human volitions, which without Him would be impotent. The idea of God and our ideational knowledge of Him are assumed in Nos. 177 and 298, and are denied in Nos. 782 and 805. Contemporary questions about God in relation to infinite space are dealt with in Nos. 177a, 290, 298, 310, 348, 391 and 825. Locke (*bis*), More, Raphson, Hobbes and Spinoza are named as thinkers who make space an attribute of God.

In notebook A Berkeley begins to think critically about the nature of God. In No. 508 he undertakes to handle the being of God as a principle of morality in his second book. In No. 625 he virtually says that if matter is, then God is matter, thus revealing the depth of his feeling for his theme and thesis. God has, or rather is, *will*, Nos. 610, 712, 812. There is no Nature over and above God; for nature is the effect of the will of God, Nos. 485, 734, 794. God is transcendent, Nos. 640, 641, and is impassible, No. 675. Our knowledge of God's existence is certain, No. 813. Berkeley has a definition of the word *God*, and he thinks it clearer than those of Descartes and Spinoza, No. 845. He does not state his definition; but we can infer the form it would take by reading entry No. 838 along with section 146 of the *Principles* and the third of the *Three Dialogues*.* The passage in the notebook specifies "unextended incorporeal Spirit . . . omniscient, omnipotent etc"; the passages from the *Principles* and the *Three Dialogues* specify, respectively, "one, eternal, infinitely wise, good and perfect" and "spirituality, omnipresence, providence, omniscience, infinite power and goodness".

* *Works*, Vol. II, p. 257.

N

APPENDIX I: TEXTUAL CHANGES IN THE DRAFT
OF THE *PRINCIPLES*, sections 85–145, made by Berkeley
for the first edition (1710)

FOUR sections, 115, 129, 132 and 140 were introduced; of these section 132 which denies that discoveries have been made by supposing infinitesimal parts of finite extensions is the only completely new one. Section 115 on seeing change of distance without knowing which body is moved, is substantially the same as three sentences to that effect which are in the Draft at the end of section 113. Sections 129 and 140 on, respectively, the infinite divisibility of the finite, and the idea of spirit in a large sense, are added on the facing page of the manuscript. As mentioned above (p. 45) Professor Jessop has noticed that section 140 in the Draft contains the words "or rather notion", crossed out. Berkeley added those very words at his revision of 1734, and was thus only restoring what he himself had written and erased a quarter of a century earlier.

Slight verbal corrections were made in sections 88, 93, and 118 of the Draft, alterations of phrasing in sections 94, 108, 122 and 145, and minor changes in sections 95, 107, 125 and 139.

Only three changes could have had a doctrinal significance: (1) in section 87 "so many sensations" was substituted for "actual sensations", (2) from the end of section 98, as drafted, two long sentences were omitted which ridicule the notion of a time wherein (a) a spirit actually exists without perceiving, (b) an idea exists without being perceived, or that there is a third sort of being which exists though it neither wills nor perceives nor is perceived, (3) from the end of section 138, as drafted, three sentences about the parts of the soul were omitted.

For further details see the *apparatus criticus ad. loc.* in Volume II of the *Works*.

APPENDIX II: THE DRAFTING PERIOD

BERKELEY began to draft the Introduction to the *Principles* on 15 November 1708 (see above, p. 45). He wrote a draft of the Principles (ss. 85–145) and made preparations for a draft of the first half (see above, p. 45). In November 1709 or early December he communicated his design and papers to his colleague, Dr. Elwood, and a month or two later he must have sent his manuscript of the *Principles* to the press. Thus a year or eighteen months elapsed between the conclusion of the *Commentaries* and the completion of the book. I call it "the drafting period".

We are not to suppose that the clock stood still during that period, or that Berkeley ceased to think; but he had more to do than speculate; he had to complete his *Essay on Vision* and see it through the press; and he had to write and re-write the *Principles*. There is no evidence, known to me, that any major development in Berkeley's thought took place during this period; on the contrary I think it is almost certain that no such development took place. The guiding lines of the *Principles* were ruled finally during the filling of the last fifteen folios of the *Commentaries*, and along those ruled lines Berkeley wrote during the drafting period.

Mr. M. F. Zeidan has written a detailed study of the drafting period, and I have had the advantage of reading it. He has compared the contents of the notebooks with those of the publications. He has, so to speak, subtracted the doctrinal content of the *Commentaries* from that of the *Essay on Vision* and the *Principles*, and drawn conclusions about what is left over. The method has its limitations, and Zeidan rather overworks the argument from silence. I find it hard to regard the silence of the *Commentaries* about the stock attributes of deity or the stock argument from dreams (*Principles*, s. 42) as significant; but I am quite ready to accept that while working at his drafts Berkeley did think out some new and not unimportant details, especially about abstract general ideas, occasionalism and Newton's laws of motion. There can be no doubt, however, that in respect of major development the period in question was one of consolidation, rather than advance.

APPENDIX III: THE REVISION OF 1734

IN 1734 Berkeley published the second edition of the *Principles* and went through that work section by section carefully with scissors and paste. No other edition appeared in his lifetime. A comparison between his revision of 1707–8, which we have been studying, and his revision of 1734 is instructive, and gives proof positive of the thoroughness and finality of the earlier revision. The revision of 1707–8 was radical, doctrinal and formative; that of 1734 was literary and verbal.

If in middle life Berkeley had wished to modify or tone down his immaterialism, he had a golden opportunity to do so in 1734. He had just kissed hands for the bishopric of Cloyne. He was at the height of his powers and his reputation. He held a leading position in the Church and in the republic of letters. His deanery, his mission to America, his *Alciphron* and now his bishopric had brought him fame, authority and responsibility. If his views on the external world had changed with the lapse of a quarter of a century and experience of life, now was the time to tell the public so. But, no. His philosophical views had not changed, and he prepared the second edition of the *Principles* and revised the work with the aim of presenting his early views in improved form and commending them to the new generation. Linguistic fashions had changed; the author's style had matured. In those respects the work needed revision and received it. There was nothing slipshod about the revision of 1734; but it was a revision of style and language, not of tenets or teaching, and it left Berkeley's immaterialism, as hammered out in 1707–8 and published in 1710, virtually unaltered.

To substantiate these statements I append the following summary account of Berkeley's revision of 1734; it can easily be checked by using Jessop's *apparatus criticus* in the second volume of the *Works*.

At his revision of 1734 Berkeley made some 237 alterations in the text. Of these about 95% are purely verbal or stylistic; there are a few explanatory insertions, and a few omissions of material no longer needed; 12 alterations call for comment—which I give below.

In his stylistic changes Berkeley has toned down the casual, conversational note which occasionally obtrudes, and has severely chastised the vague and off-hand style of arguing, confessed by the far too frequent "etc."; 41 alterations (17% of the total) merely consist in omitting "etc.", or in substituting an equivalent. Colloquial phrases like "stand to it" (section 80) are replaced by more literary language (here "assert"). Violent phrases are softened, and vigour is sacrificed to urbanity; "sceptical cant" (section 87) becomes "scepticism". Redundant statements disappear; e.g. "This is too obvious to need being insisted upon" (section 87). After "Hence it is plain, that the very notion of what is called *matter* or *corporeal substance*, involves a contradiction in it" (section 9), two sentences are omitted on "the tenent of the existence of matter". They lack urbanity and are redundant, coming immediately after the statement that the notion of matter involves a contradiction. Purely verbal changes like "comfort" for "pleasure" (section 2, Introduction) do not call for comment.

The following alterations require comment:

(1) The original Dedication and Preface were omitted; they were out of date.

(2) The compliments to Sir Isaac Newton (section 110) were toned down, and the description of him as "a philosopher of a neighbouring nation" was omitted.

(3) In the Introduction, section 16, three sentences were added accepting abstraction in the sense of considering separately separable parts. This addition merely amplifies a principle already clearly laid down in section 10, "I own myself able to abstract in one sense..."

(4) At the end of section 5 Berkeley omits the statement, "In truth the object and the sensation are the same thing, and can-

not therefore be abstracted from each other." The term *sensation* is ambiguous, and this alteration is difficult to handle briefly. I think Berkeley omitted the statement for fear readers would understand it to mean that we see our seeing, and sense our sensing. He has already said that we cannot "see or feel anything without an actual sensation of that thing"; and that is as much as to say that the object-thing and the sensation are not different. That negative way of putting it safeguards "the possibility of real existence or perception", and rules out the absolute object of the materialist. Probably Berkeley did not wish to go further and make the positive assertion of identity because of the ambiguity latent in the term *sensation*.

(5) The word "notions" is omitted from section 25, where the first edition reads, "All our ideas, sensations, notions or the things which we perceive . . . are visibly inactive." The term *notions* there is out of place. Berkeley may have intended it to designate the indirect objects of sense, and objects of memory and of the imagination; or again it may have been a vestige of his original panpsychism. His reason for omitting it in 1734 is quite plain—he is on the point of introducing a highly specialized use of the term (see No. 6 below).

(6) Significant additions about *notions* are made in sections 27, 89, 140 and 142. This is a change in terminology, but is not a doctrinal change. The aim of all four additions is to charge the term *notion* with a specialist application to objects of thought that are not *ideas* in Berkeley's technical sense, viz. spirits, mental operations and relations. Berkeley in the latter part of the *Commentaries* and in the *Principles* denied that we have ideas of God, or of the soul, or of the operations of the mind; and he never went back on that denial; he made it as strongly in 1734 as he did in 1710; but he found that those who had not grasped his use of the term *idea* misunderstood the denial; he laid himself open to a flank attack, and to meet that attack he adopted the term *notion* to describe spiritual realities as objects of knowledge. We have a notional knowledge of them, he said, though we have no ideational knowledge of them. We have no

idea of God, but we have a notion of Him. We have no idea of the soul, but we have a notion of it. The sections of the *Principles* (135 ff.) on our knowledge of God and the soul are in no way altered by the introduction of the term *notion* in the second edition; it is a purely verbal change.

(7) In section 89 spirits and ideas are contrasted, and two of the contrasting terms, used in the first edition, viz. *incorruptible* and *perishable passions*, are struck out in the second edition. The omissions do not alter the sense of the passage, nor do they weaken the contrast between spirits, described as "active, indivisible substances" and ideas, described as "inert, fleeting dependent beings". *Incorruptible* and *perishable* are complementary scholastic terms. *Passions* is an ambiguous term; in the first edition it appears to mean *passive beings*; if it meant *passive modes of mind*, it was a residuary trace of Berkeley's panpsychism.

(8) In section 101 the words "and their relations" were added to "ideas received from sense", to describe the fields of mathematics and science. The addition only makes the implicit explicit.

(9) From the opening of section 108 one sentence on the language of the Author of nature was omitted; its substance is contained in sections 44 and 66.

(10) In section 108 "rules of Nature" is substituted for "laws of Nature". The point is explained at the end of the previous section.

(11) At the end of section 115 five sentences were omitted on impressed force and absolute and relative motion, with special reference to Newton's problem of the rotating bucket, and to the question whether "one only body" could move. Those problems were, I presume, no longer topical.

(12) From the end of section 132 three sentences on fluxions and the differential calculus were omitted. Their gist is that a finite sensible quantity cannot have an infinite number of real parts. This point has been argued clearly and adequately in sections 130 and 131.

The results of the foregoing collation show that Berkeley in his fifty-first year remained convinced of the truth of the published philosophy of his youth; for when revising the *Principles* for the second edition, he made no doctrinal changes, or none of any substance. Far from abandoning immaterialism, or weakening on it, he re-affirmed it in 1734 in its full strength. The second edition of the *Principles* is simply an improved edition giving the same teaching as the first. The revision of his first arguings, carried out at infinite pains in his notebooks in 1707–8, was so thorough, so successful and so satisfactory to the author that in 1734 he found no doctrinal changes were needed.

INDEX

abstraction: false, 112; legitimate, 113; as a faculty, distinctive of man, 113; Berkeley's doctrine an afterthought, 103–7; its source, 104; entries on, 112 ff.; connection with the New Principle, 107; and words, 112; and Locke's views, 110–11; and generality, 111

Academics, 17, 29, 72

Adam, fall of, 81

Alciphron, 188, 197

algebra, 63

Almanzar, battle of, 39

Anaxagoras, 144–5

arguings: Berkeley's first, 12, 46, 148, 160; include writings, 47 ff.; and the *Philosophical Commentaries*, 79 ff.; contents of, 53

Aristotle, 132, 141, 186

Arithmetica and Miscellanea mathematica, 40, 43–4

Arnauld, 69

atheism, 67, 192

attributes, of deity, 182, 195

Bacon, 94, 117

Barrow, I., 41, 77

Bayle, P., 11, 15, 67 ff.; dictionary articles, *Anaxagoras*, 70, *Pyrrho*, 70, *Zeno*, 74, 100

Beattie, J., 12

Berkeley, Geo.: his early writings, 43 ff.; Fellowship candidate, 40; Librarian, 41; his first arguings, 46 ff.; his second thoughts, 65, 131, 138; his sceptical phases, 21, 23, 173; his dialectical method,

25 ff.; his industry, 86; his sincerity, 21

Berkeley, Wm (père), 39

body: as combinations of powers in God, 27, 32, 133 ff., 154; its nominal existence, 135; its real existence, 135; two significations of the term, 139 ff.; as effect, 154; and matter, 131; stages of development of Berkeley's doctrine summarized, 155

Bracken, H. M., 62 n.

Browne, Bishop Peter, 104

Cartesians, 17, 29, 72

certainty, 136, 152–3

Chapman MS., 45 n., 103

Cheyne, G., 77

Collier, A., 41

Commentaries, the *Philosophical*: purpose of, 58; dating of, 55; marginal apparatus, 56–7; the two notebooks, 53–4

common sense, 14, 16–18, 29, 146, 161, 167

conscious things, 83, 124, 164

consciousness, 87, 157, 161; and mind, 164

conservation, divine, 35

creation, 35; Berkeley's problems of, 140 ff.

death, 178

Deering, Mr., 48

definition, Berkeley's, of God, 193

Defoe, D., 117

deity: Berkeley's notions of, 182 ff.; space as an attribute of, 192